Property and Trust Law in Uruguay

Property and Trust Law in Uruguay

Mariana Barua

This book was originally published as a monograph in the International Encyclopaedia of Laws/Property and Trust Law.

Founding Editor: Roger Blanpain
General Editor: Frank Hendrickx
Volume Editors: Alain Verbeke & Vincent Sagaert

Wolters Kluwer

Published by:
Kluwer Law International B.V.
PO Box 316
2400 AH Alphen aan den Rijn
The Netherlands
E-mail: lrs-sales@wolterskluwer.com
Website: www.wolterskluwer.com/en/solutions/kluwerlawinternational

Sold and distributed by:
Wolters Kluwer Legal & Regulatory U.S.
7201 McKinney Circle
Frederick, MD 21704
United States of America
E-mail: customer.service@wolterskluwer.com

ISBN 978-94-035-4754-1

e-Book: ISBN 978-94-035-4764-0
web-PDF: ISBN 978-94-035-4774-9

This title is available on www.kluwerlawonline.com

The Author

Mariana Barua was born on March 24, 1979, in Lima. She studied at the University of Lima and became Juris Doctor in 2004 (with honors, Magna Cum Laude). She also attended the University of Santiago de Compostela (Spain), as an exchange student. She obtained the validation of her law degree in Uruguay. She practiced law for five years in Lima, and afterward moved to Montevideo and practiced law there ever since. She received her L.L.M. from the University of California, Davis, in 2008, and a Master's in Civil Law (with an emphasis in Contracts) at the Catholic University of Uruguay. Since 2016, she has been Professor of Civil Law (Contracts) in the University of the Republic of Uruguay. Mariana Barua is author of several articles and has contributed to several books and journals.

The Author

Table of Contents

List of Abbreviations

ART.	Artículo (Article)
ASSE	Administración de los Servicios de Salud del Estado (Health Services State Administration)
CGP	Código General del Proceso (Uruguayan General Proceeding Code)
CNA	Código de la Niñez y la Adolescencia (Uruguayan Childhood and Adolescence Code)
CP	Código Penal (Uruguayan Criminal Code)
CPP	Código del Proceso Penal (Uruguayan Criminal Proceeding Code)
DGR	Dirección General de Registros (Register General Department)
HMO	Health Maintenance Organization
IPC	Indice de Precios al Consumo (Consumption Prices Index)
JLC	Juzgado Letrado en lo Civil (Civil District Court)
SCJ	Suprema Corte de Justicia (Supreme Court of Justice)
SOA	Seguro Obligatorio de Automotores (Automobile Mandatory Insurance)
SSR	Superintendencia de Seguros y Reaseguros (Insurance and Reinsurance Superintendence)
TAC	Civil Court of Appeal
UCC	Código Civil (Uruguayan Civil Code)
UNASEV	Unidad Nacional de Seguridad Vial (National Unit of Road Security)
UR	Unidad Reajustable (Readjustable Unit)
URA	Unidad Reajustable de Alquileres (Readjustable Unit of Leases)

List of Abbreviations

General Introduction

§1. GENERAL BACKGROUND OF THE COUNTRY

I. Geography

1. Uruguay is located in a strategic geographical area in the south of South America, between Argentina and Brazil, with access to the River Plate and the River Parana, as well as to the Atlantic Ocean. Uruguay has an area of 176,215 square kilometers, and 95% of its territory has soil suitable for agriculture and livestock activities.[1] Uruguay is the second smallest country in South America, after Suriname. Uruguay shares borders with Argentina to its west and southwest and Brazil to its north and northeast. It also borders the Río de la Plata to the south and the Atlantic Ocean to the southeast. Its capital is Montevideo, and has a population of 3,440,157, of which 1,377,617 live in Montevideo (last census was conducted in 2011[2]).

2. In Uruguay, 48.34% of the population is male and 51.66% is female. Regarding the age of the population, in Uruguay, 21.42% are under 15 years old, and 13.84% are over 64 years old. And 64.74% are between 15 and 64 years old.

3. Ethnic groups in Uruguay can be described, pointing out that most of the Uruguayan citizens have white ancestors, mainly Italian and Spanish ancestors. According to the last census, 94% of Uruguayans believe they have white ancestors, 8% believe they have Afro-American ancestors and 5% believe they have Indian ancestors. Around 2% of people older than 10 years do not know how to write and read (in the rural areas, this percentage is 3%). And 2% of people living in Uruguay were born abroad. Of this percentage, most of them were born in Argentina, Brazil, Spain and Italy.

1. http://www.uruguayxxi.gub.uy/en/wp-content/uploads/sites/7/2014/10/Uruguay-profile-01.png.
2. http://www.ine.gub.uy/documents/10181/39317/Uruguay_en_cifras_2014.pdf/aac28208-4670-4e96-b8c1-b2abb93b5b13.

4. Life expectancy in Uruguay is 73 years for men, and 80 years for women. Regarding employment, in August 2021, 9.50% of its population was unemployed.[3] According to the World Bank, in 2020, Uruguay had the highest per capita income in South America.[4]

5. Since 1991 Uruguay has been a Member State of Mercosur (Mercado Común del Sur—Southern Common Market), which is an economic and political agreement that currently has five sovereign members: Argentina, Brazil, Paraguay, Uruguay (foundational members) and Venezuela (became a member in 2006 and afterward was suspended in August 2017). Bolivia is in the process of becoming a member. Chile, Colombia, Ecuador, Guyana, Perú, and Suriname currently have an associate member status.[5]

II. Cultural Situation

6. Before Spanish colonization, Uruguay was scarcely inhabited, except for some nomadic tribes, mainly the Charruas. The Spanish arrived in Uruguay in 1516. At the same time Spain started colonizing Uruguay's land, the Portuguese also advanced its colonization from what is nowadays Brazil, toward Uruguayan territory. The first Spanish permanent colony was founded in 1624, in Soriano, and the first colony of Portuguese settlers was founded in 1669 in Colonia del Sacramento.

7. Montevideo, Uruguay's capital, was founded by the Spanish in 1724, and its natural harbor soon competed with Buenos Aires harbor. Spain and Portugal fought for the region throughout the seventeenth century. Spain ultimately prevailed and established the Virreinato del Río de la Plata (Viceroyalty of the Rio de la Plata).

8. In 1810, General José Gervasio Artigas led a revolution formed by people from Uruguay and Buenos Aires, and in 1814 Spanish authorities had to leave the country, after being defeated by the revolution troops.

9. In 1815, a national government was formed. Nevertheless, in 1816 Brazilian forces invaded Uruguay and after four years of struggle, they conquered the Banda Oriental and named it *Provincia Cisplatina.*

10. On August 25, 1825, Uruguay declared its independence. After this declaration, a war took place and was called the Cisplatine War. After five hundred days of fighting, in 1828, both sides, with the intervention of the United Kingdom, agreed to sign the Treaty of Montevideo.

3. http://www.ine.gub.uy/.
4. https://datos.bancomundial.org/indicator/NY.GDP.PCAP.CD?locations=ZJ&most_recent_value_desc=true.
5. https://www.mercosur.int/quienes-somos/paises-del-mercosur/

11. After the signing of this treaty, Uruguay became an independent country. Uruguay's first Constitution was issued on July 18, 1830.

12. Currently, Uruguay is considered an attractive place to invest. According to Uruguay XXI (the Investment and Export Promotion Institute), the reasons for this are the following:[6]

- Political, legal, and social stability: Uruguay has a democratic system with institutional and legal stability, which guarantees a positive business environment and respect for the regulatory framework.
- Macroeconomic stability: In 2019, Uruguay reached the longest period of economic growth in its history, consolidating seventeen years of expansion at an average annual rate of 3.8%.
- Preferential market access: Uruguay is a member of Mercosur and has signed an FTA with Mexico. This makes it the gateway to a potential market with 550 million people.
- Investor benefits: Uruguay offers significant incentives for foreign and domestic investors, which are related to aspects such as taxes, and the free-trade zone and free port and airport systems.
- Ease of doing business: Uruguay guarantees equal treatment for investors and a restriction-free operation for business activity.
- Modern logistics: Uruguay's first-class port infrastructure, road network, and free-port system make it the best logistics platform in the Mercosur region, as well as an advantageous distribution center for goods in transit.
- Leader in ICT: Uruguay leads the ICT Development Index for Latin America (ITU, 2017). It is also the first and only country in South America to be part of D9, the group of the world's most advanced states in digital governance.
- Competitive national talent: Uruguay was the first country to implement the One Laptop per Child program. It has full digital inclusion, free education, everyday use of English and Portuguese, and a State-run university accessible to everyone.
- Efficient energy policies: Uruguay is one of the Latin American countries with the highest investment in clean energy, and it is also at the forefront of global production of electricity from wind power. In the 2017–2020 period, 97% of electricity was produced from renewable sources, 32% of which came from wind farms.
- Excellent quality of living: Montevideo has the best quality of living in Latin America (Mercer, 2019). Also, Uruguay is the country with the highest and best-distributed income in the region.
- The country's significant growth over the last decade is related to a strong increase in investments: In Uruguay, Foreign Direct Investment (FDI) has reached record levels, which has allowed the country to become one of the main FDI destinations in South America over the last decade, in terms of GDP. Investors trust Uruguay due to the profitability obtained and the good business environment, in addition to being a country with an investment grade.

---

6. https://www.uruguayxxi.gub.uy/uploads/informacion/547d1df4f16265c270cf362f1a4b51779ad0706e.pdf

- Strategic Location: Uruguay has a strategic location as a gateway to Mercosur, and two of its main ports, Montevideo and Nueva Palmira, are located at the end of the Parana-Paraguay-Uruguay river system. Its time zone, between the U.S. and Europe, makes the country a great complement to offer global services to the region and the world.
- An excellent environment for business: Laws that protect and ensure equal treatment for both foreign and local investors, a free exchange market and a single tax system throughout the country are some of the conditions that make Uruguay an attractive and safe destination for business.
- Highly attractive tax benefits: Uruguay offers a wide array of incentives adapted to the different business sectors that can be developed in the country, e.g., industry, trade, or services: (i) investment promotion system (Investment Law)—20% to 100% refund of invested amounts; (ii) free-trade zone—users are 100% tax free; (iii) temporary admission of raw materials and supplies; (iv) only South American country with free airport regime, in addition to being the only one on the South American Atlantic coast with a free-port regime.
- A country with investment grade: Uruguay is a country with an investment grade, ratified by the main credit rating agencies: Moody's, Standard & Poor's, Fitch Ratings, DBRS and R & I. Some of the reasons behind this vote of confidence for Uruguay were its macroeconomic balance and stability, an incremental diversification of the economy, and its efficient debt-management strategy.

13. Also in Uruguay clear rules can be found, taking into account that:

(1) according to Economic Freedom (2021), made by Heritage Foundation, Uruguay is ranked 2nd in South America and is ranked 44th in the overall ranking;[7]
(2) according to Political Stability (2020), developed by World Bank's Worldwide Governance Indicators, Uruguay is ranked 20th and 1st in terms of Political Stability in Latin America;[8]
(3) according to the Corruption Perception Index (2020), prepared by Transparency International, Uruguay is ranked 21st out of 180 countries and is the 1st country in Latin America in terms of reliability and low levels of corruption[9].
(4) finally, the Global Competitiveness Index (2019), made by the World Economic Forum, places Uruguay as the 3rd most competitive country for business in Latin America, after Chile and Mexico, and is ranked 53rd[10] in the overall ranking[11].

14. Finally, we deem it important to point out that the magazine *The Economist* chose Uruguay as its 2013 "Country of the Year."

---

7. https://www.heritage.org/index/country/uruguay
8. https://www.theglobaleconomy.com/rankings/wb_political_stability/
9. https://www.transparency.org/en/cpi/2020/index/ury
10. https://www.theglobaleconomy.com/rankings/davos_competitivenes_new_measure/
11. https://www.theglobaleconomy.com/rankings/davos_competitivenes_new_measure/Latin-Am/

III. Political System

15. Uruguay, after its independence, was organized politically as a Democratic Republic with a State formed by nineteen departments: Artigas, Canelones, Cerro Largo, Colonia, Durazno, Flores, Florida, Lavalleja, Maldonado, Montevideo, Paysandú, Río Negro, Rivera, Rocha, Salto, San José, Soriano, Tacuarembó and Treinta y Tres, with Montevideo as the capital city. The Uruguayan Constitution is the basis for all other statutes, and its modification requires the affirmative vote of two-thirds of the total of the members of the House of Representatives (Cámara de Diputados) and of the Senate (Cámara de Senadores). It can also be modified with the approval of a national referendum. The Uruguayan Constitution can be accessed—in Spanish—in this site: http://www.impo.com.uy/bases/constitucion/1967–1967.

16. The guiding principles of the Uruguayan Constitution are the following:

- the republican principle;
- the democratic principle;
- the principle of legality;
- the separation of powers principle (Legislative, Executive and Judicial Powers).

17. The republican principle is established in Articles 1, 2, and 3 of the Uruguayan Constitution and refers to a form of government in which monarchy is prohibited. The democratic principle is established in Article 82 of the Uruguayan Constitution and states that the Nation's sovereignty belongs to the citizens, who directly or through elected representatives will practice it, through the enactment of the laws that will govern them.

18. The principle of legality is established in Article 18 of the Uruguayan Constitution, and states that the law will determine the order and formalities of the trials in Uruguay.

19. The principle of separation of powers is established in section IV of the Constitution, in which the Executive Power, the Legislative Power and the Judicial Power are described.

20. The Executive Power has a structure in which the head is the President. The President is elected along with the Vice President for a five-year term. The President cannot be reelected after the end of the five-year term, but can run for presidency again after another president is elected and finishes his administration.

21. To win an election, a candidate has to obtain more than 50% of the citizens' votes. In case this percentage is not obtained, the first and second most voted candidates will compete for the Presidency.

22. The President appoints the Ministers, which are the head of the Ministries, which in Uruguay are thirteen: National Defense; Social Development; Economy and Finance; Education and Culture; Farming, Cattle Raising and Fishing; Industry,

Energy and Mining; Defense; Foreign Affairs; Public Health; Work and Social Security; Transportation and Public Constructions; Tourism and Sports; Housing, Land Use Planning and Environment (more information about Uruguayan Ministries, http ://ministerios.gub.uy).

23. The Legislative Power is administered by the Uruguayan General Assembly, which is formed by two Chambers: the Chamber of Senators (Senadores), which is composed of thirty senators, and the Chamber of Representatives (Diputados), which is formed by ninety-nine representatives. Senators and Representatives are elected for a five-year term, and can be reelected. The Legislative Power website is www.parlamento.gubuy, and it has, among others, a database in which legislation can be consulted.

24. Uruguay has also local governments, one in each of its nineteen departments. Each local government has a Governor (Intendente), which represents the Executive Power of the Department, and a Local Assembly (Junta Departamental), which is the Legislative Power of the Department. The website of the local government of Montevideo is www.montevideo.gub.uy.

25. In 2009, the Alcaldías were created in towns in which more than five thousand inhabitants lived. These Alcaldías are committees with five members, where one of them is the President. Additionally, Montevideo has been divided into regions, and Alcaldías have been created for each one of them.

26. Currently, the President of Uruguay is Luis Lacalle Pou, who took office on March 1, 2020.

§2. Legal Background of the Country

I. Legal Family or Tradition

27. Uruguay belongs to the civil law systems, with its roots in the Napoleonic Code and the Roman law.

II. Relation and Hierarchy Between the Sources of Law

A. Sources of Law

28. Uruguayan law has four sources: legislation, custom, case law, and the settled/official view among academics.

29. Legislation or statutory law is the group of legal rules issued by a competent authority of the State.[12] Under the term "legislation," we understand it comprised the law issued by the Legislative Power, as well as the decree of the Departmental Council, or the decree passed by the mayor or Executive Power.

30. In Uruguay, legislation is the only formal source of law. When a legal rule takes the form of legislation, meaning that it is passed by a competent authority, it is mandatory.

31. The second source of law is custom. The customary law is the law that is formed unconsciously among a society, after the repetition of the same practice time and time again, and due to the conviction of this society that this repetition is necessary and mandatory.[13] Custom is, therefore, formed by two elements: a material element—the use or repetition of an act—and another psychological element—the certainty that this act is binding and that its violation will result in a punishment.

32. This practice must be general, and constant, and perceived as mandatory. Some authors have sustained that for a custom to legally exist, case law must apply it. Therefore, according to them, if several judicial rulings apply the custom, then it becomes a legal custom. This opinion has been disregarded by most authors, who argue that when a judge issues a ruling, he applies a rule of law: he does not create the rule; he only applies it. Therefore, for the case law to apply custom, it first has to exist legally.

33. Custom is very important for Uruguayan law because it nurtures law with social reality. Social reality varies depending on the historical moment and place, and therefore, in a way, custom updates law. Nevertheless, as was already said, in Uruguay, custom is not a formal source of law.

Indeed, Article 9º or the Civil Code states that: "It is not possible to abrogate statutory laws with other statutory laws; and it will not be possible to allege against its abidance the lack of use or the custom or practice against it. *Custom does not constitute law unless in cases in which a statutory law refers to it* (Article 594, numeral 2)" (emphasis added). Therefore, in cases in which legislation refers to a custom, the custom (material source) will give content to the statutory law (formal source).[14]

34. As an example of a law that refers to a custom, we can mention numeral 2 of Article 594 of the Civil Code, regarding the dividing wall between two buildings. This article states the following: "The height of the dividing line will be determined by the regulations that may exist, *and by the custom* which should be constant and well-known" (emphasis added).

---

12. *See* Vescovi, Enrique, "Introducción al Derecho," 17th edn Montevideo, Idea, 1992, pp. 72–73.
13. *See* Vescovi, Enrique, "Introducción al Derecho," *supra*, pp. 73–78.
14. The Civil Code can be found—in Spanish—at http://www.impo.com.uy/bases/codigo-civil/16603-1994.

35. Therefore, it can be established that in Uruguayan law, following the trend of the French Revolution, statutory law has an absolute predominance, and even in cases of legal loopholes, judges are not authorized to recur to custom (which is an option that has been adopted by the most modern codes).

36. The third source of law is case law. Case law has been defined as "the way in which laws are interpreted by Courts," or as "a group of judicial rulings issued regarding a specific issue."[15] When there is a loophole or doubts regarding the interpretation of a law, judges, when applying it, must give their position and when the thesis is repeated (in several rulings), it is said that there is "case law."

37. Strictly speaking, it would be enough with only one ruling, to be able to state that there is case law regarding a matter (and in case this ruling is embraced by other Courts, it would become a "leading case").

38. Without prejudice to this, in Uruguayan law, jurisprudence (case law) is not a formal source of Law. The ruling of a judge in a certain case does not compel other judges, even when they have a lower position. This opinion does not force judges at all. Even the same judge can rule differently in a future case regarding the same issue at hand, without having to explain this change of opinion.

39. The rule that states that in our country case law is not a formal source of Law is Article 12 of the Uruguayan Civil Code (UCC), which states: "Only the legislator can explain or interpret the law in a generally mandatory way. Judicial rulings are not binding in other cases different to the case in which they were issued."

40. It is also important to point out that Article 14 of the UCC establishes that: "The High Court of Justice, anytime it deems it convenient, will inform the Legislative Power of the doubts and difficulties that occur in the intelligence and application of the law and about the loopholes perceived in them, in order to encourage, either the interpretation of the existing statutory laws, or the passing of new laws." Therefore, although case law is not a formal source of law, the High Court of Justice can perform acts in order to improve legislation, through the communication to the lawmakers of the difficulties found when applying statutory law to specific cases.

41. Notwithstanding the aforementioned, in Uruguay (as well as in other civil law countries), despite the leeway judges have to rule as they deem fair, they are increasingly influenced by case law. This trend has caused that more and more editorials publish case law, and that the Judicial Power creates an online database with all rulings of the Appellate Court and the Supreme Court, in order that judges and lawyers can find out the trends of case law regarding a specific case.

42. Another source of law is the settled/official view among commentators or academics. Article 16 of the UCC states that in case of loopholes, judges must resort

15. *See* Vescovi, Enrique, "Introducción al Derecho," *supra*, p. 78.

to the most received opinions of academics (and when this happens, the opinion of academics becomes a material source of law). Indeed, Article 16 of the UCC states that: "When a civil act occurs, and it cannot be solved by the words or by the spirit of law in the matter at hand, the grounds of analogue laws should be considered, and if even then the doubt subsists, the general principles of law and the opinion of academics should be considered, taking into account the case circumstances."

It is important to point out that, even though the opinion of academics is not a formal source of law, Legislators as well as judges are always aware of the opinion of the most important academics of Uruguay and abroad, and frequently, Legislators use these opinions as inspiration for new laws, and judges use them in order to justify their rulings. The most received opinions of academics in Uruguay are the ones of Professors Jorge Gamarra, Juan Blengio, Carlos De Cores, Jaime Berdaguer, Beatriz Venturini, and Dora Szafir, among others.

43. Finally, the last source of law is the General Principles of Law. As was already said in point 43, Article 16 of the UCC states that these principles can be applied when a civil act occurs and it cannot be solved by the words or the spirit of law. The Supreme Court of Justice (SCJ) in its ruling 246/2002 dated 9/9/2002 has stated, citing other authors, that these principles are "Guidelines that inform to a law and inspire directly or indirectly a series of solutions for which they can be used to promote or guide the approval of new rules, advise on the interpretation of the ones in force, and resolve the cases not foreseen by laws" (Plá Rodríguez, "Los principios del Derecho del trabajo," 2a. Ed., pag. 9), and that "To solve an unforeseen matter in accordance with the general principles means, therefore, to rule as the lawmaker would have, in case he could have had knowledge of this specific case" (García Maynez, "Introducción al estudio del derecho," pág. 372).[16]

B. Sources of Private Law

44. As was already said, in Uruguay, the law can be divided into public and private law. Private law is also divided into different branches of law: civil law, commercial law, etc. Civil law can be divided as well in patrimonial and extra patrimonial law. Extra patrimonial law studies the individual and its personality, as well as family relations, while patrimonial law (which is called in Common Law Private Law) refers to the law of contracts and torts (as it is called in the Common Law), or the law of obligations (as it is called in civil legal systems). Therefore, sources of private law (or civil patrimonial law) are studied in Uruguay as the sources of obligations.[17] In this sense, when referring to obligations, the word "source" means "efficient cause," i.e., "what gives origin to an obligation."[18]

16. *Vazquez, Jose y otros v. CUTCSA,* SCJ No. 246/2002 (2002).
17. *See* Peirano Facio, Jorge, Curso de Obligaciones, Tomo I (1957), pp. 33–38.
18. Berdaguer, Jaime, "The Obligation," Vol. I, Editorial Fundacion de Cultura Universitaria, Montevideo, p. 59.

45. Obligations, as will be seen afterward, can refer to a civil wrong that causes someone else to suffer loss or harm resulting in legal liability for the tortfeasor, or as a legal duty that arises from a mutual agreement or from law. In this case, the breach of this duty will give place to the legal liability of the breacher.

46. Article 1246 of the Civil Code states that "Obligations rise, from mutual assent of two or more individuals, as in the contracts, from a voluntary act of the individual obliged, as in the quasi-contracts; due to an act that has given place to harm or damage to another person, as in the crimes and quasi-crimes, or when the law states it, as in the family relations, or in the civil relations. Obligations that rise from law are expressed in it."

47. Therefore, it can be established that there are five sources of obligations: the contract, the crime, the quasi contract, the quasi crime, and the law. Historically, the contract is the oldest source of the obligation. Although the crime happened before the creation of the contract, the contract was identified as a source of obligations first. The quasi contract is another source of obligations. In this case, there is an unlawful act that generates an obligation, but in which the meeting of minds is lacking. Another source of obligations is the quasi crime, in which the offender does not have the will to commit the crime (unlike what happens when a crime is committed). Finally, the fifth source of the obligation is statutory law. Besides obligations, or civil wrongs that arise from the abovementioned sources, statutory law refers to other obligations that appear from special circumstances, and that when breached generate civil wrongs.[19]

48. Therefore, regarding the sources of obligations in Uruguayan law, we can find acts or sources that are normally intentional: the contract and the crime. There are also two sources which are non-intentional: the quasi contract and the quasi-crime. There are two sources which are legal: the contract and the quasi contract, and two that are illegal: the crime and the quasi-crime. And in the middle, giving symmetry to all of this, appears the statutory law.[20]

§3. Introduction to the Law of Property and Trust

49. In our Civil Code, as also happens in the French Civil Code, there is not a chapter destined to regulate property. Furthermore, our Civil Code, as well as the French Civil Code, only as an exception, uses the word "property." Usually, the Uruguayan codifier refers to property as assets, and when referring to all the belongings of a person, he refers to "the assets and rights" (e.g., Articles 777, 880, 1043, and 2265 of the UCC). An example of this is the ruling SEI 0005-000071/2014,

19. *See* Peirano Facio, Jorge, Curso de Obligaciones, Tomo I (1957), pp. 33–38.
20. *See* Peirano Facio, Jorge, Curso de Obligaciones, Tomo I (1957), pp. 33–38.

dated 8/13/2014, of the Civil Court of Appeal, in which the Court states: "the patrimony of the debtor is composed by his assets and rights, and by the joint property assets and rights (…) except those assets and rights that are not subject to seizure."[21]

I. Historical Origins and Evolution

50. Property has the same origins in Uruguay as it has in other civil law countries. Its origins are in Rome, in which this concept was created and studied. In Roman law, a division was made between: people, things, and actions, which influenced one way or another, in all the future classifications.

51. From these classifications, the actions were separated from the other two categories, in order to configure the civil procedure area. Anyhow, in our Civil Code and in all modern Civil Codes, dispositions which refer to actions remain, which are a reminiscence of this first classification.

52. Also, in all codes and projects of codes drafted before ours, after a preliminary title, in which general issues are treated, a first book is dedicated to "People," and a second book is dedicated to "assets," or, as our Civil Code points out: to assets and domain or property.[22]

53. It is also important to point out that, since the independence of Uruguay, property has been understood as an inviolable right. Indeed, Uruguayan Constitution of 1830, in Article 7, states that "The inhabitants of the Republic have the right to be protected in the enjoyment of their life, honor, liberty, security, job, and *property*. No one can be deprived of these rights except according to the laws which are established for reasons of general interest."

II. The Concept of Ownership

A. *Unity and Fragmentation*

54. Our Code transmits an idea of property which is naturally linked to the idea of individual property. It also refers to the idea of condominium, but shortly, and it treats it as a right which is not provided with the continuity of individual property. The Civil Code deals poorly with the relationship among the residents of a condominium, and when it does, it is in order to point out ways that allow them to put an end to this situation, and enter a situation of individual property. Property, seen this way, is considered the first and more important of the rights regulated by the Civil

21. Pedro Santana S.A. c. Shepley, TAC 2, SEI 005-000071/2014 (2014).
22. Iglesias, Arturo, "Derecho de las Cosas," Tomo I, Editorial Fundación de Cultura Universitaria, pp. 7–8.

Code. It is also the right to which more protection is provided, and that only exceptionally can give way to other possible conflicting rights.[23]

55. Property regulated by the Civil Code refers to property of material goods. Article 491 of the Civil Code states that special laws will regulate productions of talent or inventiveness. Also, property such as horizontal property, funerary property, mining property, and industrial property is regulated outside our Civil Code.

56. In the Roman tradition systems (as ours), property is based on the possession of things, or it is based on abstract forms of possession, such as the possession secundum tabulas, to which systems, following mainly Germanic influence, transferred the function of publicity to the registry.

57. All the types of property that are not regulated in the Civil Code will have their own rules, and will not be ruled by all or part of the essential principles of property of the Civil Code.

58. Currently, the forms of landownership regulated in Uruguayan law are the following: absolute freehold (propiedad plena), limited freehold (propiedad limitada), life estate (derecho real de por vida), Commodatum (comodato), lease (Arrendamiento), joint ownership (propiedad indivisa), usufruct (usufructo), and bare ownership (nuda propiedad).

B. Immovable and Real Property (See Also Part I)

59. Uruguay's law distinguishes between movable (muebles) and immovable (inmuebles) property, the criteria being whether they can be displaced/transported or not (with some exceptions, such as airplanes). They are regulated by Uruguay's Civil Code, in Articles 460–470.

60. Uruguay's Civil Code in Article 463 states that immovables are the things that cannot be transported from one place to another, such as land, mines, and buildings. Article 464 states that trees and plants are also considered immovables, as long as they are fixed to the land through their roots. The fruits of the plants and trees will also be considered immovables, and will belong to the owner of the land.

61. Article 465 states that the things destined for the use, farming and benefit of an immovable will also be considered immovables, such as linings, water pipes, animals destined to help in a farm, compost, and machines destined to be used for farming.

62. However, according to Article 466, the products of the immovables, and the things accessory to them, such as herbs, wood and fruits, soil or sand, metals of a

23. Iglesias, Arturo, "Derecho de las Cosas," *supra*, pp. 14.

mine or the stones of a quarry, are considered movables, even before their separation, in order to establish a right in favor of the other person different from the owner.

63. Regarding the things attached to the walls, Article 467 of the UCC states that the things that provide comfort or beauty, and that are attached to the walls, if they can be removed easily, are considered movables. But, if the paintings or mirrors are attached to the walls, in a way that they become a part of them, they are considered part of the building, even if they can be separated from the walls without damaging them. The same is applicable to statues which are placed in a niche build for this purpose in the wall.

64. Regarding things which are accessories to real estate, Article 468 or the Civil Code determines that they will not cease to be part of such real estate if they are separated momentarily from it, but they will cease to be part of them if they are separated with the purpose of giving them a different destiny.

C. *Movable and Personal Property* (See Also Part II)

65. Uruguay's Civil Code in Article 462 states that movables are the things that can be transported to another place either because these things can move by themselves (such as animals) or because they can be moved by others. The Civil Code excludes from this category those movable things which are destined to the use, farming, or benefit of an immovable.

66. Article 470 of the Civil Code distinguishes movables as perishable and non-perishable. The first refers to those things that cannot be used according to their nature, without being consumed. Money in all its forms is considered perishable because it perishes for he who uses it.

III. Estate and Patrimony

A. *Unity and Fragmentation*

67. In Uruguay, the Uruguayan State has the obligation to protect Uruguay's inhabitants in their right to property. Indeed, as was already pointed out, since the independence of Uruguay, property has been understood as an inviolable right. This is why, the Uruguayan Constitution, in Article 7, states that "The inhabitants of the Republic have the right to be protected in the enjoyment of their life, honor, liberty, security, job, and *property*. No one can be deprived of these rights except according to the laws which are established for reasons of general interest."

68. Also, Article 492 of Uruguay's Civil Code establishes that "No one can be deprived from his property, being it movable or real estate, without a cause of public utility, determined by law." And in the case of public utility, previously to taking away the property, the State must compensate the owner.

69. Nowadays, private property is necessary for the development of an individual. People need to fulfil their basic needs, such as food, clothes, and housing. Private property also allows that people can start their own businesses and consume goods and services, and therefore allows the economy to grow, generating the country's welfare.

70. The patrimony of an individual also serves as a guarantee for his obligations before third parties. Indeed, Article 2372 of the Civil Code states that "The patrimony of the debtor, except regarding those assets which are not subject to seizure, is the common guarantee of his creditors, and its price will be distributed among them pro rata, unless there are legitimate causes of preference. The law does not acknowledge other causes of preference, but the pledge, the mortgage and the privileges."

71. When we refer to an individual's patrimony, we refer only to his or her assets, although it can also be understood as the assets minus the debts of the individual. It is not necessary that a person be present in order to have a patrimony. Indeed, Article 52 of Uruguay's Civil Code refers to the patrimony of a person who is missing. It is also not necessary for a person to be an adult, in order to have a patrimony. Indeed, the patrimony of children subject to *patria potestas* is regulated in Article 267 of Uruguay's Civil Code.

72. Another thing to point out regarding an individual's estate is that it is not possible to donate all of it to third parties. This prohibition applies even if he restricts the donation to his estate at the time of the contract (and not to the things and rights he might acquire in the future) (this is established by Article 1625 of the Civil Code).

73. However, an individual can donate his estate, as long as he keeps a minimum amount, for his basic needs. In all cases, a donation will be void if it refers to the future things or rights to be acquired by the individual. It is also forbidden to donate during life more than one can give by will (Article 1626 of the Civil Code). Therefore, the entire estate of an individual can only be given away after he dies, and if the diseased has heirs, he can only donate the portion of free disposal (*see infra* Part III, Chapter 3).

74. Another prohibition is that an individual cannot divide his patrimony in a way that some of it is not available for his creditors. If an individual becomes shareholder of a company and transfers all his estate to it, he will become the owner of shares that will represent the value of this estate (although the estate transferred becomes property of the company).

75. Also, if an individual gets married and does not sign a prenuptial agreement by which separation of estates is agreed or if afterward, before a judge, does not ask for the separation of their estates, then a community of estates regime will apply to the estates of the spouses from the date of the marriage. In this case, during the time the community property regime is in force, the creditors of one of the spouses can seize his property, as long as it was owned by him before getting married. The community property estate can also be seized if it is administered by the debtor spouse (Article 1975 of the Civil Code). Also, in the latter case, half of the estate subject to seizure will have to be reimbursed by the debtor's spouse to the nondebtor's spouse, in case the marriage is dissolved.

76. Other important issue to take into account when analyzing the estate of a person refers to the inheritance. In Uruguay, there are two ways in which a person can inherit: with the benefit of inventory or without it. If someone inherits with this benefit, then he will be liable for the debts of the deceased only up to the value of the deceased estate. But if he accepts the inheritance without using this benefit, then he will be liable for all the debts of the deceased, even with his own patrimony (Articles 1069 and 1092 of the UCC).

77. In Uruguay, it is also possible to incorporate corporate vehicles, in order to separate a person's own patrimony from the patrimony of the company. The company can have the form of a Corporation, or it can be a Limited Liability Company, the two most popular options.

B. *Trust and Fiduciary Mechanisms* (See Also Parts IV and V)

78. In Uruguay, there is another way to achieve "patrimonial fragmentation." Indeed, through a trust, a person can introduce part of his patrimony in a legal entity, in which this patrimony can be administered for his benefit.

79. Caffera defines the contract of trust as a contract in which an obligational relationship is created between the trustor and the trustee. The trustor agrees to establish a fiduciary property of things and rights and to pay a compensation to the trustee, unless otherwise agreed. The trustee agrees to comply with the instructions of the trustor, for the benefit of the beneficiary.[24]

80. Trusts are regulated in Uruguay, by Law 17.703, which defines the trust as "a legal transaction by which a fiduciary property of a group of property rights or other real or personal rights, are transmitted by the trustor to the trustee, so that he can administer them, or use them according to the trustor instructions, in benefit of other person (the trust beneficiary) who is appointed in the Trust. The trustee will have to return the fiduciary property after the period of time established for the Trust

24. Caffera, Gerardo, El contrato de Fideicomiso, análisis de la ley Uruguaya 17.703, Asociación de Escribanos del Uruguay, 2003, pp. 18.

is over, or after the requirement established in the trust has been achieved, returning it to the trustor, or giving it to the trust beneficiary. There can be more than one trustor and beneficiary."

81. In Uruguay, trusts are especially used in the construction area. They are also frequently used as a guarantee.

IV. Possession and Title

82. In Uruguay, real rights have an erga omnes efficacy. But in order for this efficacy to be opposable to people, different from the contracting party, this right must be registered in the Public Registries. This way, the said right will have the necessary publicity. In Uruguay, it is possible to register real rights, when they refer to immovable property, as well as to some kind of movable property, subject to registration, such as vehicles.

83. In the case of movable property, which does not have a register in which the ownership can be registered (automobiles, ships, among others, do have this registry); possession will be the way to give real rights publicity. Possession can be defined as the control an individual exercises toward a thing. The UCC defines possession as "having a thing or enjoying a right by ourselves and with the intention of an owner, or when another person has it or enjoys it on our behalf" (Article 646 of the Civil Code).

84. The person that has the possession of something will be presumed its owner, unless proven otherwise. As the presumed owner, he will be able to defend the property in Court, by taking legal actions (Article 649 of the UCC). This article of the Civil Code also provides that the person that has the possession of something in a peaceful and public way, during one year, without being interrupted in his possession, will not have to prove that he is the owner, with a title deed.

85. If a person purchases a stolen movable property, without knowing this situation, the buyer will have to return the property to he who proves to be the real owner. But if a person buys a movable property in a public place, or from a seller that makes a living selling this type of things, the real owner cannot recover his property without previously paying the price of the purchase (Article 1213 of the UCC).

86. Finally, by possessing a thing, it is possible to obtain the property of it. If the possessor has possessed with a title deed and good faith, he has to prove to have possessed for three years to obtain the ownership of the movable property (Article 1212 of the UCC). However, if the possessor has possessed without a title deed and without good faith, he will have to prove possession during six years, in order to become owner of the property. This is known in Uruguayan law as acquisitive prescription (or usucapion) (Article 1214 of the UCC).

Part I. Immovable Property and Real Property

Chapter 1. General Classification

87. In Uruguay, property is not divided—as it is in the Common Law—between real and personal property. In Uruguay, property is divided into corporal and non-corporal property (Article 460 of the UCC).

88. Among corporal property, we can find movable and immovable things. Non-corporal property is divided into real and personal rights. Real rights refer to the rights we have regarding a thing (i.e., possession, property, etc.), or against a thing (i.e., a mortgage) (Article 472 of the UCC), while personal rights are the rights we have regarding other people (i.e., the right to collect a debt) (Article 473 of the UCC). Real rights can be opposed to everyone (erga omnes effect), while personal rights can be opposed only to the person with which one has contracted.

89. The Civil Code divides personal rights into three categories: depending on the obligation consists in giving, doing or not doing something (Article 1245 of the UCC). Real rights will vary depending on the powers the beneficiary has in relation to the property.

90. Besides the real right of property, there are other so-called minor real rights, which produce an effect that does not refer to the transfer of the property. Such minor real rights are divided between the minor real rights of enjoyment (the usufruct, the easement, and the right of use and habitation) and the minor real rights of guarantee (pledge, mortgage and the right that arises from the registration of the contract of promise of transfer of real estate to be paid in instalments, and of the promise of transfer of real estate or of commercial establishment).[25] The real right of guarantee becomes effective after its registration.

91. While the property right gives the owner powers to use, enjoy, modify and dispose of the property (Article 487 of the UCC), the minor real rights are always compatible with the property right, and do not give the titleholder such wide powers.

---

25. Gamarra, Jorge, Tratado de Derecho Civil Uruguayo, Tomo VIII, 52 (Fundación de Cultura Universitaria ed., Montevideo, 2010).

92. In Uruguay, property prolongs during the life of the owner, and after its owner dies, it is inherited by the owner's heirs. Meanwhile, minor real rights have most of them an expiration date. Indeed, usufructs can last at the most during the lifetime of the usufruct beneficiary. If the usufruct is given to an entity, it can last, at the most, thirty years (Article 501 of the UCC). The right of use and habitation can also be given, at the most, for the lifetime of the beneficiary (Article 500 of the UCC).

93. Property as well as some limited real rights can affect realty or chattels. Most of the real rights are regulated by the Civil Code. Nonetheless, there are some real rights regulated by other laws, such as the pledge without dispossession (Law 17.228), easement of water (Law 14.859, which regulates the Code of Waters), among others.

94. In Uruguay, it has been discussed the possibility to create new real rights. Some authors understood that the list of real rights of the UCC was "Numerus clausus" (a closed list), while others understood it was "Numerus Apertus" (an open list) and that, due to this, new real rights could be created by the parties.[26]

95. This discussion came to an end after Article 17 of Law 16.871 stated that "The following will be registered in the Real Estate Section of the Property Register: 1. The public instruments in which it is established, recognized, modified, transferred, declared or extinguished the dominium, use, right to live in a property, surface right, easement, any dismemberment of the dominium, mortgage, census and the rest of real rights established by law over immovable goods." After this law, all authors agreed that the list of real rights was a Numerus Apertus list.

96. Finally, while personal rights have their origin in contracts, quasi contracts, crimes, quasi-crimes or in the law (Article 1246 of the UCC), real rights have their origin in the law, in contracts, and they can also be obtained through succession instruments, accession, occupancy and usucapion.

26. Iglesias, A, El número de los derechos reales, la superficie y los derechos de adquisición, Anuario de Derecho Civil Uruguayo, T. XXV (Fundación de Cultura Universitaria ed., Montevideo), pp. 623–642.

Chapter 2. Legal Interests

97. In Uruguay, unlike Common Law countries, we do not differentiate between "legal interests" and "equitable interests." In Uruguay, property as well as minor real rights are considered legal interests because they are regulated by law, and they are opposable to everyone (erga omnes effect). But in order to have this erga omnes effect, real rights must be registered in the Public Registry.

§1. Property National Registry Function in Uruguayan Law

98. In Uruguay, the function of the Registries is to make public the acts and transactions that the law deems important, which can be summed up in two fundamental aspects: the registration of the acts and the provision of information when it is requested.

99. Law 16.871 regulates the organization and functioning of the Public Registries. The authority in charge of supervising the correct functioning of the Public Register is the Dirección General de Registros (Register General Department (DGR)). This Department depends on the Ministry of Education and Culture, but has technical autonomy.

100. The Public Register is divided into the following registries: Property National Registries, Personal Acts National Registries, and Commerce National Registries.

101. Regarding the Property National Registries, each one of Uruguay's nineteen "departments" (provinces) has a property registry covering that Department. It is located in the Department's capital. The registry does not issue a copy of the deed; rather, a certificate with the information of key elements: buyer, seller, price, and date recorded.

102. The registry is public, so anyone can have access. Anyone (notary or not) may request information by filing a form and paying a small stamp duty. The prior deeds are also kept with the rest of the documentation, and they can also be found in the registry ledger of the notary who authorized them.

103. The notary public ("escribano") is who conducts a search and examination of title for conveyancing and financing. For the conduction of a complete search, separate sub-repositories must be reviewed for certain records, e.g., deeds, mortgages, leases or judgments. The local convention for the time frame of a real estate title search is of twenty years (the time needed to prescribe rights, through possession).

104. Once the transaction has been agreed, the parties go to a notary who will prepare a deed, which the parties will sign, and the notary will authorize. Afterward, a minute is prepared by the notary, who submits it for recording, together with the deed. The registry then returns the deed, with the official recording stampings.

105. Between the moment the parties sign the purchase agreement and the recording of the deed, some time may elapse. That time lapse is, usually, of one to three days. To ensure that nothing can affect such transfer, the buyer's notary previously records (and the registry places) a "priority reservation" on the property, for thirty days. If it expires, the notary can ask for a new one.

106. The legal effect of the records in the registry on third parties consists in the enforceability of the recorded right to a third party. The concept is known as "oponibilidad." So, for example, if a third party purchases a property and it has a recorded mortgage, that mortgage affects the property regardless of the third party's transaction.

107. The forms of business organizations and other entities that are competent to hold title to real estate in the country are the following: individuals, civil entities (asociacion civil), and corporate entities (sociedad comercial: SA, SRL, Sociedad en comandita por acciones), foundations and trustees (on behalf of a trust). On the other hand, the organization that cannot hold title in its own name is the trust. In it, the property is held by the trustee.

108. Note that there is also a restriction for rural land affected by rural activity (as opposed, for example, to mining or development activity): it cannot be owned by a corporate vehicle whose share/quota holders are not individuals and whose shares are not nominative (as opposed to bearer-type), unless a special exception has been granted by the Executive Power.

109. Also, it is important to point out that the entities organized in foreign jurisdictions are competent to hold title to property. Indeed, it is common to see entities such as Delaware LLCs, Panamanian corporations and BVI entities holding properties in Uruguay.

§2. Immovable Property

I. Concept, Characters, and Social Function

110. Article 486 states that the domain (also called property) is the right to enjoy and dispose of a thing arbitrarily, as long as it is not against the law or the rights of others.

111. The Civil Code divides things into corporal and incorporeal. As was already said in §2, II, among corporeal things, the Code distinguishes between movable (muebles) and immovable (inmuebles) property, the criteria being whether they can be displaced/transported or not. They are regulated by the UCC in Articles 461–470.

112. Uruguay's Civil Code in Article 463 states that immovables are the things that cannot be transported from one place to another, such as land, mines, and buildings. Article 464 states that trees and plants are also considered immovables, as long as they are fixed to the land through their roots. The fruits of the plants and trees will also be considered immovables, and will belong to the owner of the land.

113. As was already mentioned in paragraphs 61–64, Article 465 states that the things destined for the use, farming and benefit of an immovable will also be considered immovable, such as linings, water pipes, animals destined to help in a farm, compost, and machines destined to be used for farming.

114. However, according to Article 466, the products of the immovables, and the things accessory to them, such as herbs, wood and fruits, soil or sand, metals of a mine or the stones of a quarry, are considered movables, even before their separation, in order to establish a right in favor of other person different from the owner.

115. Regarding the things attached to the walls, Article 467 of the UCC states that the things that provide comfort or beauty, and that are attached to the walls, if they can be removed easily, are considered movables. But, if the paintings or mirrors are attached to the walls, in a way that they become a part of them, they are considered part of the building, even if they can be separated from the walls without damaging them. The same is applicable to statues which are placed in a niche build for this purpose in the wall.

116. Regarding things which are accessories to real estate, Article 468 of the Civil Code determines that they will not cease to be part of such real estate if they are separated momentarily from it, but they will cease to be part of them if they are separated with the purpose of giving them a different destiny.

117. After distinguishing between movable and unmovable property, the Code refers to incorporeal things, and states that they can be personal (when they can be claimed by other persons) or real rights (when we have the right regarding a thing or against a thing).

118. The Civil Code refers to the right of property in general, except for some special kinds of properties (such as intellectual property, property on water or joint ownership, which are regulated in other laws). In Uruguayan law, property is the most comprehensive right (it gives the most extensive powers over a thing), it is perpetual (it is not conditioned by a period of time), and it is opposable to third parties (erga omnes).

119. In the UCC, the owner has the right to enjoy a thing, as long as this enjoyment does not go against the law or the rights of others, granting the owner (Article 487) all the powers over the thing, even the power to destroy it. This concept of property failed in the twentieth century, when social needs made it necessary to limit this power. An example of this was the law of leases (Law 14.219, passed on July 22, 1974), which established, among other dispositions in the detriment of the lessor, obligatory minimum periods of time for leases, which in case of personal use were of two years, and for industry and commerce were of five years.

120. The Uruguayan Constitution of 1967 embraced this principle of protecting the right of property, but taking into account the public need, and therefore in Article 7° states that "the inhabitants of the Republic have the right to be protected in the enjoyment of their life, honor, liberty, security, work and property," and afterward says that "no one can be deprived from these rights unless according with the laws established for reasons of general interest."

121. Also, Article 32 of the Constitution states: "The property is an inviolable right, but is subject to what is established by the laws enacted for reasons of general interest. No one can be deprived of his right to property unless in the cases of public necessity or public utility, established by a law, and receiving always from the National Treasure a just and previous compensation (…)."

II. The Defense of Property

122. Uruguayan law establishes different ways of protecting property. The principal mechanism for protection of property is called vindication, and is regulated in Article 676 of the UCC. According to this article, "the owner has the right to pursue in trial the property of his thing, against anyone that possesses it and pretends to withhold it. The action he will have in this case is called vindication, or action of dominion."

123. Therefore, vindication is an action the owner has against the person who tries to appropriate a thing he owns. The plaintiff must prove the following: (a) that he is the owner of the thing; (b) that the defendant is in possession of the thing claimed; and (c) the identity of the thing claimed.

124. Besides vindication, there are also other actions, which can be carried out to obtain judicial protection for the right of possession. Article 658 of the UCC calls possessive actions those actions that aim to maintain or recover the possession of real estate or real rights established over it.

125. Article 661 of the UCC states that the person that has been disturbed in his possession or unjustly deprived of it has the right to ask to be protected, or that the property or right be restored, along with a compensation of trial costs, expenses, and other damages. This action has a statute of limitation of one year since the disturbing act occurred, or after the property or right has been unduly deprived (statute of limitations). If the new possession was violent or clandestine, this period of time will start when the violent or clandestine act stops.

126. Another thing to point out about this action is that when it is directed against the former possessor, the plaintiff must prove that he has possessed in a peaceful and public way for at least one whole year. In the remaining cases, the plaintiff will only have to prove that he was in possession of the property at the moment of the disturbance or deprivation.

III. Urban Property

127. Although, as was said before, in Uruguay, owners of property have a wide range of powers regarding the thing owned, urban property is one of the cases in which property is limited by different regulations. Indeed, legal stipulations regarding urban land establish in detail where a person can build, what he can build, the number of floors that can be built, etc.

128. Currently, the statutory regulations of urban property are comprised in the Law of Territorial Ordination and Environment (Law 18.308) recently enacted on June 30, 2008. This law divides land into three categories: urban land, suburban land, and rural land.

129. Urban land category comprises the areas of territory of the populated centers, the ones destined for residential development, with the infrastructure and all services provided, as well as those areas subject to residential development that are only partially urbanized, in which it is planned to maintain or complete the urbanization process.

130. In the urban land category, the instruments of territorial ordination can determine the following subcategories: (a) consolidated urban land category, when it refers to areas of land urbanized, which have at least a potable water supply system, drainage system, paved roads, sewage evacuation system, electric energy and streetlight; (b) nonconsolidated urban land category, when it refers to areas in which, even existing a minimum of infrastructure, it is not sufficient. Also, this category refers to the zones deteriorated or with lack of use that should be modified in order to become consolidated.

131. Finally, the suburban land category comprises the areas of land where there are settlements with uses, activities, and installations of an urban kind, or zones in which this type of activities prevail, which are dispersed in the territory, or contiguous to a populated center. The installations and constructions typical of the suburban land category are the following: habitable, touristic, residential, related to sports, recreational, industrial, for the rendering of a service, logistic or similar.

132. Land is also regulated by the dispositions of each of the Department Municipalities. In application of Article 8 of the law, so far, 92 instruments of territorial ordination have been approved and 114 are being drafted. They refer to Departmental Guidelines, Local Plans, Programs for Coordinated Action and Sectorial Plans.[27]

133. The possibility to build is regulated in both the national law and the departmental laws approved by each Municipality. These laws establish which land must be protected from urban construction, which land must be considered urban, and which one rural, as well as the way in which construction must be carried out (where can a commerce establishment can function and what places must only have residential buildings).

IV. Agrarian Property

134. According to Article 31 of Act 18.308, the rural land will comprise the areas of territory that the territorial ordination instruments establish as rural, including the following subcategories:

(a) Rural productive: This category comprises territory areas whose principal destiny is the agrarian activity, livestock, forestry or similar, mining or extractive, or those which the territorial ordination instruments establish to secure the availability of the productive soil and the areas in which this soil prevails. It can also comprise as rural soil the territorial zones with the aptitude to be used for rural production, when it refers to areas with conditions to be destined for agrarian, livestock, forestry or similar uses, and are not yet being used for this.
(b) Rural natural: This category comprises the areas of protected territory, with the purpose to maintain the natural environment, biodiversity, or to protect the landscape or other patrimonial, environmental, or spatial values. It can also comprise the streambed of the lagoon, lake, collection, and the watercourses of public or fiscal domain, of the territorial sea, and of the coast defense belt.

135. The territories of the rural land category are excluded from any process of urbanization and residential development.

136. The Uruguayan Rural Code (which was approved by Law 10.024, dated June 14, 1941) also regulates agrarian property and refers to it as a "Rural Establishment." This Code states on Article 283 that "to the effects of this Code, it is understood as a rural establishment, any real estate property that, located outside the common land, and in lack of this, outside the suburbs of the cities, villages or villas, is destined or can be destined to the raise, improvement or fattening of cattle, or to farming."

27. https://sit.mvotma.gub.uy/inot/

137. This Code regulates, among others, that rural establishments must comply with the following:

(1) The obligation to demarcate the property with milestones, which must be visible and cannot be separated by a bigger distance than 1 kilometer among them (except when the limit is a river or a stream) (Article 3).
(2) The owner must have the blueprints of the property, registered in the General Cadastral Office and the National Real Property Administration, Office of Topography and Regional or Municipal Technical Inspections, in order to transfer part of the property or to divide it (Article 7).
(3) The obligation to fence the property, after being authorized to do so by the municipal authority (Article 8).
(4) The wire fence must have seven wires, and the distance between the posts cannot be bigger than 15 meters.

138. It also states in Article 285 that the owner of a rural establishment will be represented by the person who appears in charge of it, and that none of the stipulations of the Code can be infringed, due to the absence of the owner in the rural establishment.

139. It is also important to point out that in Uruguay, a Code of Water (Decree-Law No. 14.859) has been enacted, which regulates the use of the water, among others, in rural properties (for the raising of cattle and for farming purposes).

140. There is a restriction for rural land affected by rural activity: it cannot be owned by a foreign corporate vehicle; it must be owned by a local vehicle, with nominative shares and individuals as shareholders (unless an exception is granted by the Executive Power). This is not a restriction to foreign ownership: the Uruguayan entity owning the land can be 100% foreign owned.

141. Another requirement is established by Article 35 of Law 11.029, which determines the obligation of a rural landowner, of land above 500 hectares, to offer the land to the National Colonization Institute (INC), before selling it to a third party, granting this way a first refusal. The offer must be under the same terms and price offered to the third party. In case the owner does not make this offer, the sale of the land becomes void, and the owner will have to pay a fine equivalent to 25% of the cadastral value of the land. The other parties involved in the transaction, as well as the notary, will be subsidiary liable for the payment of this fine. Regarding the right established in favor of the National Colonization Institute, Dr. Camaño states that "the interpretation and application of this regulation must be analyzed in a restrictive way, being excluded from it the analogy or extension, due to the fact that this regulation generates a restriction to the individual right of property, protected by the Constitution."[28] The INC rarely makes use of this right since it is a public body with limited funding.

28. Camaño Iriondo, Mario, "El derecho de preferencia del art. 35 Ley 11.029," en Revista de Derecho Agrario, No. 4, p. 34.

Regarding this right of first refusal, the first Civil Court of Appeal ruled in a leading case in which the seller decided not to sell his property, after being notified of the interest of the INC of buying it. In this case (ruling No. CED-0003-000997/2013 dated 11/21/2013),[29] the INC filed a lawsuit so that the Court ordered the owner of the land to sign the purchase deed. In this case, the Court understood that Article 35 of Law 11.029 granted the INC a right to acquire the property of a land, in case the owner decided to sell it to a third party. Therefore, the law stated the obligation of the owner to inform this institute of his intention of selling, before signing any agreement with the third party. It did not state the obligation of the owner to offer to sell the property to the INC. Therefore, in cases like this, if the INC informs the owner that it wants to buy, it does not modify or substitute an existing contractual bond. Therefore, when the owner offers the land to the INC, and the INC informs its intention of buying, this does not generate the formation of a purchase agreement. The purchase agreement will only exist after the purchase deed is signed. Therefore, according to the Court, Article 35 establishes a right of first refusal, but does not give the INC the right to force the selling of the property against the owner's will.

142. Another restriction to the right of property is established in Article 477 of Law 13,640, by which MEVIR (which is a public person of private law, that lends money to people with few resources, for the construction or improvement of houses in rural areas) has a right of priority over the properties it builds or improves, in virtue of which, when the owner of said property agrees to sell it, he first has to offer it to MEVIR (in the same price and conditions), who can decide to purchase it instead of the other interested party. This priority right comes to an end when the owner completes the payment of the money lent by MEVIR for the construction or improvement of the property.

29. *Instituto Nacional de Colonización v. Fitesur S.A.*, TAC 1, No. CED-0003-000997/2013 (2013).

Chapter 3. Equitable Interests

143. As was already mentioned in paragraph 98, in Uruguay, unlike Common Law countries, we do not differentiate between "legal interests" and "equitable interests." In Uruguay, property as well as minor real rights are considered legal interests because they are regulated by law, and they are opposable to everyone (erga omnes effect), but in order to have this erga omnes effect, real rights must be registered in the Public Registry.

Chapter 4. Limited Interests

§1. Usufruct

I. Concept, Setting-Up, and Statutory Provisions

144. Diez-Picazo defines usufruct as a real right, which grants its owner a right regarding specific things, and therefore generates a specially protected situation toward third parties.[30] According to Article 493 of the UCC, usufruct is the real right that consists in the enjoyment of another person's thing, with the obligation to keep its form and substance, and to give it back to his owner, if the thing is not fungible, or to return the same quantity and quality of the same kind or to pay its value, if the thing is fungible. Usufruct supposes necessarily two coexistent rights: the right to the bare ownership of the thing and the right to enjoy the thing. Therefore, it has a limited duration, after which the right to enjoy the thing goes to the bare owner, and the property consolidates.

145. Statutory provisions of the usufruct are established in Articles 493–540 of the UCC. These provisions refer to its definition (493–493), the ways to establish a usufruct (494–501), the rights and duties of the usufructuary (502–532), the rights and duties of the owner (533–536), and the ways to put an end to the usufruct (537–540).

146. The parties will determine the rights and duties of the usufructuary. Only in case those rights and duties are not established, Articles 502–532 of the UCC will apply (this is determined by Article 494 of the UCC).

147. Article 495 of the UCC states that a usufruct can be established by law, by an agreement between living parties, by last will acts and by prescription (Articles 266, 269, 497, 1619 and 1664).

148. If the usufruct is established through an agreement between living parties, the right to enjoy the thing is not acquired until it is delivered or handed over, according to the rules of title III of the Third Book of the UCC.

149. If the usufruct is established as a last will, the right to the thing is acquired after the testator passes away. The usufruct is acquired by prescription, in the same way as the dominium and is subject to the same set of rules.

II. Subjects and Object

150. The person that benefits from the usufruct is called the usufructuary, which can be a natural person, a village, a corporate body or a public establishment.

30. Diez-Picazo, Luis, and Gullon, Antonio, "Sistema de Derecho Civil," Vol. III, 7th Edition, Editorial Tecnos, p. 326.

151. When the usufruct is established in favor of a natural person, it can be established to last during the lifetime of the usufructuary. If it is established in favor of a village, corporate body, or public establishment, it cannot be established to last for more than thirty years. In this case, the usufruct will terminate before the thirty years if the village becomes deserted, the corporation dissolves, or the public establishment is suppressed (Articles 500 and 501 of the UCC).

152. A usufruct cannot be established in favor of two or more natural persons, so that they can enjoy a thing alternatively or successively (Article 498 of the UCC). Nevertheless, it can be established this way if it is agreed that these persons must enjoy it simultaneously, in equal parts, or according to the quotas determined by the grantor (Article 499 of the UCC).

153. The usufruct can be established, with no conditions, under a condition or since or until a specific day. When a period of time is not established, it must be understood that the usufruct must last for the lifetime of the usufructuary (Article 500).

154. The bare owner is the owner of the thing subject to usufruct. He can perform, even against the usufructuary's will, all the acts necessary for the conservation of the thing. He can also transfer his bare ownership (Articles 534 and 535 of the UCC).

155. On the other hand, the owner of the thing cannot do anything that alters the enjoyment of the thing by the usufructuary. He also cannot alter the state of the thing, not even improve it (Articles 533 and 534 of the UCC).

156. The usufructuary must pay the periodic burdens and taxes related to the use of the thing during the time he enjoys it (Article 525 of the UCC). The burdens and taxes referred to the value of the thing must be paid by the owner (Article 526 of the UCC). He must also pay for the minor repairs of the thing, required for its conservation (Article 523 of the UCC).

157. Regarding the object, the usufruct can be established regarding movable or immovable things, a group of things (e.g., an inheritance) or quotas of co-ownership. Normally usufruct is established regarding productive and non-fungible things. Nevertheless, the UCC expressly regulates the case of a usufruct established in a consumable thing (Article 507).

158. In this case, the usufructuary becomes the owner of these things, and the bare owner becomes a simple creditor of the usufructuary, who will have to deliver him other things of the same quantity and quality, or the value of them at the time the usufruct is over.

III. Content

159. Unless agreed otherwise, the usufructuary has the right to use and enjoy the fruits or profits of the thing given in usufruct, which can be natural, industrial or civil (Article 502 of the UCC). Natural fruits are the spontaneous produce of the land, the offspring, and other products of the animals. Industrial fruits are the ones produced by the estate, after being cultivated or after working in it. Civil fruits are the rents of the estates and the interest of the money.

160. The usufructuary can perform improvements in the thing subject to usufruct, but he will not have the right to be reimbursed for the money spent on these improvements. Nevertheless, he can compensate this amount with the amount owed due to the deterioration of the thing. The usufructuary can also remove the improvements from the thing, as long as this removal does not cause harm to it (Article 512 of the UCC).

161. The usufructuary can rent the thing, transfer his right over it, even free of charge, but all the contracts that the usufructuary signs will terminate at the time the usufruct finishes (Article 511 of the UCC).

162. Regarding the obligations of the usufructuary, the UCC establishes that before starting enjoying the thing, he must: (i) make a solemn inventory of the things received, valuing the movables and establishing the state of the immovables; (ii) give a security that guarantees that he will take care of the things as a good family father, and will return them to the owner at the time the usufruct is over, without harming them due to negligence (Article 514 of the UCC). This last duty will be excluded in case of legal usufructs, in case the donor reserves the usufruct of the thing donated, and in case the owner or the grantor of the usufruct disposes of so (Article 515 of the UCC).

IV. Extinction and Liquidation

163. The usufruct comes to an end when the following happens (Article 537 of the UCC): (i) when the usufructuary dies; (ii) when the time of its duration finishes, or when the resolutory condition occurs; (iii) when the consolidation of the usufruct with the property occurs; (iv) due to the lack of use, according to the rules of prescription; (v) when the usufructuary renounces to this right; or (vi) due to the real and complete destruction of the thing subject to usufruct.

After the usufruct comes to an end, the things subject to usufruct must be returned to the bare owner.

Finally, it is important to point out that in case law, it is common to see cases in which the creditors of the owner of a thing claim the simulation of contracts in which the owner sells a real estate property, and agrees with the buyer the usufruct of the thing during his life.

For example, in the ruling 127/2011 dated 05/25/2011, issued by the second Civil Court of Appeals,[31] the plaintiff alleged that his debtor simulated the sale of his house, in order to avoid its seizure by his creditors. In the sale, it was agreed that the seller would have the usufruct of the house during the time he lived. The Court understood that this was a simulation, and that what really was agreed between the seller and the buyer was the donation of the house. With this ruling, in Uruguay, it is easier for the plaintiff to ask the Court to declare the nullity of the contract, due to the fraud of the plaintiff (acción pauliana, Article 1296 of the UCC).

§2. Building and Planting Rights

I. Concept

164. In Uruguayan law, the right to build or plant on other person's land is called the right of surface (derecho de superficie). This right refers both to the right to build in urban land and to the right to plant in rural land.

165. The UCC does not regulate the surface right (derecho de superficie). Notwithstanding this, some authors allege that the right of surface can be deduced from Articles 749 and 751 of the UCC.

166. Article 749 of the UCC states that: "all the works, sowing and plantations made in a land, are presumed to be made by the owner at his expense, and they belong to him, if not proven otherwise," while Article 751 of the UCC points out that: "The owner of a land in which another person, without him knowing it, had built planted or sowed, will have the right to appropriate the building, the plantation or the sown field."

167. Lanziano Washington[32] affirms that "articles 749 and 751 of the UCC, although they do not establish the right of surface, (…) they show that the principle of accession is not absolute, although it has been categorized among those of public order." And afterward, citing Salis,[33] he says: "Salis, (…) when considering the acquisition by accession and the institute of surface, says that: 'this connection between both things, soil and construction, can be broken, according to our laws, only by two ways: through the separate transfer of the existent building, or by the establishment of a right of surface'."

31. *García Silvera, Ivonne Graciela v. García García,* María del Carmen; y otra, TAC 2, 127/2011 (2011).
32. Lanziano Washington: Estudios de Derecho de superficie y Propiedad Horizontal, pág. 6, cited by Susana Cambiasso, in her article "El Derecho de superficie en el Derecho Uruguayo," published online at: http://secretarias.unc.edu.ar/acaderc/doctrina/articulos/el-derecho-de-superficie-en-el-derecho-uruguayo.
33. Salis Lino, Superficie (Diritto vigente). En Novisimo Digesto Italiano. T. XVIII. Pág. 948, cited by Lanziano Washington: Estudios de Derecho de Superficie y Propiedad Horizontal, *supra.*

168. Meanwhile, the conveyance attorney (notary) Susana Cambiasso understands that "although it would not be necessary that a law established and said expressly that a right is real if it has all the features of it, the law must reveal those features. Evidently, Article 751 does not establish the features of a legal surface right in favor of the owner of the building, although Garcia Goyena alleges that this was written based on a similar article of the Spanish Civil Code. Article 751 reveals the property by blueprints as an exception to the accession." The property by blueprints refers to the case in which in a vertical projection of a building several owners can exist.

169. The surface right was first established expressly in the Registry Law 16.871. Indeed, Article 17 of Law 16.871 stated that "The following will be registered in the Real Estate Section of the Property Register: 1. The public instruments in which it is established, recognized, modified, transferred, declared or extinguished the dominium, use, right to live in a property, surface right, easement, any dismemberment of the dominium, mortgage, census and the rest of real rights established by law over immovable goods."

170. Nevertheless, this right was already used by the conveyance attorneys in Uruguay, in the horizontal property regime. It was frequent that the owner of a land built a horizontal property, kept one unit, and established a surface right over the land, so that he could build in the spare land.

171. After Law 16.871 expressly recognized the surface law, in 2008 Law 18.308 was enacted, and in it, the surface right was for the first time regulated. Indeed, Article 36 of this law states: "The owner of a real estate, private or fiscal, can grant to other the surface right of his land, for a period of time, freely or with a cost, through a public deed that must be registered, and through the delivery of it (tradition)."

172. After saying this, Article 36 of Law 18.308 defines the surface right in the following way: "The surface right is the limited real right established over someone else's real property, that grants temporarily part or all of the property and comprises the right to use the property according to the general stipulations of the legislation, within the frame of the instruments of territorial ordination, and according to the respective contract. The holder of the surface right will have, regarding the property, the same rights and obligations as the owner of it."

173. Finally, the said law states that, after the surface right is extinguished, the owner will recover the full dominium of the real estate, as well as of the accessions and improvements made to the property, unless agreed otherwise in the contract.

174. It is important to point out that, although the surface right is meant to be temporary, the law does not establish a maximum period of time for its duration.

175. Authors understand[34] that the right of surface can be subject to mortgage, as well as the property of the owner (although in the latter case, the creditors will have to wait for the surface right to finish, in order to auction the property).

176. Finally, regarding case law, one case we deem interesting to comment regarding the surface right is the ruling 26/2014 dated 2/28/2014, issued by the sixth Civil Court of Appeals,[35] in which the plaintiff asked the Court to order the occupants of the property to deliver it to him, after having bought it in an auction. The defendant argued that he had a surface right over the property, and that the mortgage of the property (constituted before the surface right) was only over some buildings of the land, and not all of them. The Court understood that due to the fact that the mortgage of the land was constituted and registered before the surface right, the defendants had to deliver the property with all its buildings, which were now property of the new owner.

II. Urban Building Right

177. This refers to the limited real right that allows its holder to build on another person's land, and become the owner of the building for a period of time. This right, in Uruguayan law, is called the surface right, and was already explained in paragraphs 187–189.

III. Rural Planting Right

178. The rural planting right is the right given to a person, to sow seeds or plant crops on another person's land, acquiring the ownership of the products sown or planted, for a period of time. The same rules of the Urban Building Right, referred to in paragraphs 187–189, apply to this right.

IV. Rights of Building Additional Floors and Sub-building

179. Articles 1 and 2 of Law 10,751 (Horizontal Property Law) allow that different persons own different floors of a building. All of them will be at the same time co-owners of the common spaces of the building.

---

34. Fernandez Reyes, Jorge, "El Derecho de Superficie en la Ley de Ordenamiento Territorial y Desarrollo Sostenible y la Materia Agraria," Published in CADE Doctrina y Jurisprudencia 345, online version, 7/6/2010.
35. Winterbotham Fiduciaria S.A. y otro c/ Loygreen S.A., TAC 6, No. 0006-000026/2014 (2014).

§3. Leasehold Interests: Chattels Real (*See Also* Part II)

180. The contract of lease consists of a contract by which a person uses someone else's property for a period of time, in exchange of a price. Statutory provisions on leases are contained first in Articles 1776–1830 of the UCC, which regulate, in general, the lease of goods, being them movable or immovable. This contract is also regulated in Law 8,153 which regulates the contract of lease in general; Law 14,219, which regulates the lease of buildings destined for housing, industry or commerce, with construction permits requested before June 1968; and Laws 14,384 and 16,223, which regulates rural leases (farming, livestock, or forestry).

181. Several authors have discussed the nature of the contract of lease. The principal scholar in civil law in Uruguay, Jorge Gamarra,[36] understands that the delivery of the thing to the lessee grants him the mere possession of the thing and not a real right over the thing or against it. He bases his opinion in Article 653 of the UCC, which establishes that "It is called mere having of the thing, that of the leasee, seizor, borrower, pledge creditor and the others that have a thing acting on behalf of another. The possession belongs to the person in which name they have the thing."

182. It is also important to point out that for the contract of lease to be opposable "erga omnes" (against all), it is imperative that the contract be registered.

183. Indeed, Article 54 of Act 16,871 (Registry Organic Law) states that "the acts, legal transactions and decisions from the competent authorities that are registered according to this law, will be opposable to third parties since the filing of the request of registration before the Registry (…)."

184. The contract of lease is a bilateral and onerous contract. And according to the UCC, it does not require fulfilling any formality, in order to be valid. Indeed, Article 1776 of the Civil Code establishes that "The lease is a contract by which two parties bind themselves reciprocally, one to grant the use or enjoyment of a thing (…) and the other to pay for this use, enjoyment (…) a specific price. The one who receives the price is the lesser, and the one who pays is the lessee. The lease becomes in force after the mutual agreement of the parties."

185. Notwithstanding this, the agreement referred to the term must be made in a written document, in order to bind the parties (Article 1786 of the UCC). Also, Law 14,219, which regulates leases of properties destined for housing, commerce, and industry establishes in Article 119 that urban leases must be executed in writing.

186. When the contract of lease refers to properties destined for housing, industry or commerce, Law 14,219 will apply as long as the lease refers to a building

36. Gamarra, Jorge, "Tratado de Derecho Civil Uruguayo," Vol I, Fourth Edition, Editorial Fundación de Cultura Universitaria, Montevideo, p. 312.

built before June 1968, or in case the construction permit of the building was requested before June 1968, and as long as the lease is not excluded by Articles 28 and 114 of this law. When the land is located in rural areas, and destined for farming, livestock, or forestry, then Law 14,384 and Law 16,223 will apply. In both cases, the rules of the Civil Code (Articles 1776 to 1855) will apply as a default rule. Nonetheless, these rules will be the main statutory provisions in the case of urban properties, with a construction permit requested after June 1968, in the case of properties excluded by Articles 28 and 114 of Law 14,219, and in general, in the cases not comprised in these laws.

I. Urban Leases

A. *Special Statutory Provisions*

187. In Uruguay, there are several laws that regulate the lease of things. First, there is the UCC (which in its current wording contains rules of Narvaja (author of the UCC) and others, included by Law 8,153). Also, there are two statutory regimes: Decree-Law 14,219 and Decree-Law 14,384 (and the laws that modify them).

188. Regarding urban leases, Decree-Law 14,219 and the UCC are the laws that apply. As was already said, Decree-Law 14,219, which establishes a protectionist regime, only applies to contracts signed after its coming into force, and regarding buildings for which construction permits were requested, or that were built, before June 1968. Also, Articles 28 and 114 of this law exclude some properties from the application of this law.

189. Therefore, in Uruguay, there are two regimes for the leases referred to housing, commerce, and industry. On the one hand, there is the protectionist regime of Law 14,219 and its modifying laws, and on the other hand, there is the free-contracting regime, in which the parties can establish freely the contractual clauses.

190. Law 14,219 sought to facilitate the use and enjoyment of the properties located in urban or rural land, subject to lease, and destined for housing, commerce, or industry. Also, Law 14,219 establishes two kinds of leases. One refers to the housing leases, and the other to industry and commerce leases.

B. *Law 14,219*

191. Article 117 of this law states that this is a law of public order, and therefore, it is not possible that parties agree against its dispositions. This law forbids agreeing to the price in foreign currency.

192. This law accepts that the definition of the contract and its content is established by the Civil Code. But it moves away from it in some aspects, especially regarding price and terms.

193. In the Civil Code, the price of the lease can be paid with the fruits of the property leased, or with money. And being paid with money, it can be agreed to be paid in national or foreign currency. Whereas, in Law 14,219, the rent must be paid only with money, and in national currency. Nevertheless, the parties, as occurs also in the UCC, can establish the price of the rent freely, and they can also agree on periodic increments of the price. Notwithstanding this, the increment can only occur every twelve months, and the adjustable unit can only be one of three options: the readjustable unit (UR), the readjustable unit of leases (URA) or the consumption prices index (IPC). At the moment, the increment is applied to the price, even though having agreed to apply another readjustable unit, the lessee can choose the lower readjustable unit (between the UR and the URA) (legal readjustment) if it turns out more convenient for him. But the lessee has only one chance to do it, and after choosing the legal regime, he cannot back out.

194. Regarding the term of the contract, the parties can establish any term within the maximum legal limits established by Article 1782 of the UCC (which states as maximum limit, the period of fifteen years, except some exceptional cases in which the properties are destined to collect water, produce energy or afforestation, among others, in which the maximum period will be of thirty years). Nevertheless, Law 14,219 also establishes a minimum limit for the term of the leases. In the housing leases, the minimum lease term is of two years (and can be extended for one more year), and in industry and commerce leases, the minimum lease term is of five years. These minimum terms bind the lessor, not the lessee. During the term of the lease, it is not possible for the lessor to ask for the return of the property from the lessee, even in case the lessor needs it for personal use, nor is it possible for the lessee to return it before the end of the term, unless he pays the price of the months left until the end of the term of the contract (Article 1785 of the UCC).

C. *Law 19,889*

195. The Law for Urgent Consideration (Law 19,889) established a new regime for urban leases, different from the one established by Law-Decree 14,219, and different from the one regulated by the CC. In this new type of lease, the parties cannot establish the obligation of the lessee to offer a guarantee to the lessor. As compensation for this, the periods for eviction are shorter than in the other regimes.

196. This new regime will only apply to the residential leases, when the lessor does not ask for a guarantee, the contract is in writing, and the parties agree to the term, amount of the rent and that this regime will apply (Article 444).

D. *Content of the Right*

197. Article 1776 of the Civil Code establishes that "The lease is a contract by which two parties bind themselves reciprocally, one to grant the use or enjoyment of a thing (…) and the other to pay for this use, enjoyment (…) a specific price.

The one who receives the price is the lessor, and the one who pays is the lessee. The lease becomes in force after the mutual agreement of the parties."

198. The lessee cannot use the leased property to other destiny than the one agreed upon by the parties. If the parties did not agree regarding this, the lessee must give the property the destiny for which it was made, or the destiny that can be presumed from the circumstances of the contract, or of the countries custom. If the lessee does not comply with this, the lessor can ask for compensation and the rescission of the contract, or only for the compensation (Article 1812 of the UCC).

199. Other duties of the lessee are to act as a good family father in the conservation of the property, and to pay the price agreed upon by the parties. The payment of the price or rent must be made in the periods agreed by the parties, or if it was not agreed, according to the custom of the country, which is within the first ten days of every month (Article 1815 of the UCC).

200. If a price has been fixed and the lessee did not pay the rent, after being demanded the payment, the lessor can ask for the resolution of the contract and the sanction established by numeral 1° of Article 1823 of the UCC, which consists in the payment of a compensation, and of all the rents due until the end of the contract. But first the lessor must demand the payment, and two rents must be owed by the lessee—if the period for the payment of the rent is at most every three months. If the period agreed for the payment is of more than three months, then it will suffice that the lessee owes one rent.

201. After the end of the contract, the lessee must give back the property in the same conditions in which it was delivered, taking into account the deterioration generated by its normal use and enjoyment. If the contract does not establish the condition in which the property has been delivered, it will be presumed that the lessee received the property in good conditions, and he must return it in the same conditions, unless proving otherwise. If the property suffered damages during the term of the lease, the lessee must prove that they were not caused due to his negligence, nor due to the negligence of the persons for which he responds (family, guests, dependents or subtenant), unless in case the damages were caused by force majeure (Article 1827 of the UCC).

202. The lessee must pay for the deterioration that according to custom occurs due to the use of the property by the lessee and its dependents. These repairs are basically those that seek to maintain the property in the same state in which he received it, but he will not respond to the deterioration occurred due to the passing of time, due to the normal use of the property, or due to force majeure, or to the bad quality of the building. The lessee should especially preserve the integrity of the walls, flat roof, pavement, and piping; replace the broken glass of the windows, doors, and partition walls; and maintain the functioning of the doors, windows, and locks (Articles 1818–1820 of the UCC). In the remaining cases, the repairs must be paid by the lessor (Article 1807 of the UCC).

203. The UCC does not allow the lessee to make improvements without the consent of the lessor, but if he makes them, the lessor is not obliged to pay for them, and the lessee can take them with him, as long as this does not cause harm to the property (Article 1808 of the UCC).

204. Also, according to Article 477 of Law 13,640, when MEVIR, which is a public person of private law that lends money to people with few resources, for the construction or improvement of houses in rural areas, builds a property, or makes improvements to a property in favor of the owner of it, its owner cannot lease (or perform any act of disposition of said property) without the authorization of MEVIR. This right comes to an end when the owner completes the payment of the money lent by MEVIR for the construction or improvement of the property.

205. In case the lessor sells the leased property, the lease will be opposable to the buyer (which will subrogate in the contract as the new lessor) only when the contract of lease has been recorded in the Property National Registry (Article 54 of Law 16,871—Organic Registry Law).

206. If the term of the lease finishes and the lessee continues in the use and enjoyment of the property leased, it will not be understood that the term of the contract is renewed. The finished contract will continue under the same terms, until the time in which the lessor asks the lessee to return the property. And he will have the right to ask for it at any time. Also, the bails, as well as pledges and mortgages established by third parties, will not extend to the obligations generated after the end of the term of the lease (Article 1790 of the UCC).

207. Notwithstanding this, in the cases that fall within Act 14,219, at the end of the term of the lease, if the parties do not celebrate a new contract, the contract will be renewed for one more year, unless the property is destined to commerce or industry. This renewal will operate automatically, after the lessee does not deliver the property in the date agreed (Article 4 of the Act). Also, after the renewal term comes to an end, the lessor can ask for the eviction of the property in a term of one year (Article 5 of the Act).

E. Registration

208. As was already mentioned, the Organic Registry Law, in its Article 17.15, establishes that the lease and sublease can be registered in the Immovable Section of the Property National Registry. After its filing in the registry, these contracts will be opposable to third parties, including, among them, an eventual buyer of the property (Article 54 of the Act).

209. But if the contract is not registered, in case the property is sold, the new owner will not be bound by the term of the contract agreed, and can ask for the eviction of the lessee at any time (Articles 1786 and 1792 of the UCC).

F. Extinction

210. The lease contract can extinguish due to multiple causes:

(a) The end of the term of the contract: This is the normal way to finish the contract. According to Article 1782 of the Civil Code, the maximum term that can be agreed is fifteen years. Nevertheless, Article 1 of Law 18.666 states some exceptions, in which the term of the contract of lease will be of thirty years, which are when the properties are used to support dams, collect water or produce electric energy, or when they are destined to forestry. The agreement referred to the term must be made in a written document (Article 1786 of the UCC). After the term of the contract comes to an end, the lessor must ask for the eviction of the lessee, who will have one year to leave the property (the eviction is regulated by Law 14,219 and applies also to the cases governed by the UCC).
(b) Unilateral rescission: After the end of the term of the contract agreed by the parties (Article 1790 of the UCC), or in case the parties did not agree a term for it (Article 1789 of the UCC), the lessor can ask the lessee to return its property, and if he does not comply, he can ask for the eviction of the lessee. In the case of properties that fall within Act 14,219, the lessee, after the end of the term of the contract agreed, can opt to renew the contract for one more year, and after this term, the lessor can ask the lessee to return the property (Article 5 of the UCC).
(c) Death: This contract is not a contract intuito personae (this expression means that the contracting parties cannot be changed because the contract is made in express consideration of the persons involved). Therefore, not being an intuito personae contract, death is not a cause for the extinction of the contract.[37] Indeed, Article 1783 of the UCC states that "The rights and duties that arise from the contract of lease are transferred to the heirs of the lessor and lessee. In the case of lease of immovables, the successors of the lessor as heirs or legatees will have the same rights and duties of them. The term does not bind the heirs of the lessee." Therefore, if the lessor passes away, his successors will assume the quality of lessors and the contract will remain in force, while, if the one that dies is the lessee, his successors can continue or not with the contract of lease, arising a right to terminate the contract unilaterally.
(d) Breach of contract: Practically, all of the obligations that arise from the contract of lease have been considered by the legislator as principal obligations (obligations of not disturbing, using the property with diligence, paying the rent, etc.) and due to this, the breach of any of these obligations by one party will give the other the right to rescind the contract.
(e) Supervening impossibility: Articles 1805 and 1806 of the UCC state cases in which the impossibility to use and enjoy a thing, such as the case of destruction of it or its expropriation, generates the rescission of the contract. But if the

---

37. Venturini, Beatriz, Barua, Mariana, and others, "Manual de Contratos I," Editorial of the University of Montevideo, Montevideo, 2011, p. 506.

destruction is partial, then the lessee can choose between rescinding the contract and continuing it with a discount on the agreed price of the rent.

II. Rural Leases

A. *Special Statutory Provisions*

211. In Uruguayan law, rural leases received a specific treatment late in time. The decision to regulate this contract aside from the lease contract was due to the acknowledgement that in the lease of things it suffices that the lessor allows the use and enjoyment of the thing by the lessee, while in the rural lease, this use and enjoyment must be wide enough for the lessee to be able to use the rented thing in a productive way.

212. In the beginning, this contract was ruled by the same statutory provisions as the lease of immovables in general. The first Rural Code in Uruguay (enacted in 1875) only regulated some aspects of the rural lease, which were already established in the UCC. The second Rural Code, enacted in 1942, and currently in force, included specific statutory provisions for the rural lease, and also regulated the sharecropping.

213. In 1975, Law-Decree 14,284 entered into force, and regulated in depth the rural lease, the sharecropping, the livestock capitalization and the shepherding, among other rural contracts. Nowadays, the statute provisions that regulate the rural lease are the UCC, Law 8,153, the Rural Code of 1942, Law-Decree 14,284 and Law 16,223. These provisions regulate specifically the use and enjoyment of a productive property for a price in money or in fruits for a period of time.

B. *Content of the Right*

214. Article 2 of Law-Decree 14,284 sets forth the content of this right, establishing that: “Every contract by which one of the parties binds to grant the other the use and enjoyment of a rural property to be destined to agriculture, livestock or agriculture and livestock, and the other party binds to pay for this use or enjoyment a price in money or in natural fruits or products of the property, it will be ruled by this law.” Therefore, for this law to apply, the contract must refer to a rural property, and it must be destined for agriculture, livestock farming or agriculture and livestock farming purposes.

215. Scholars have questioned the rules for lease contracts of properties destined to agriculture, livestock, or both, when they are not located in rural areas. The most accepted position states that in these cases, the UCC will apply because Law 14,219, which regulates urban leases, excludes expressly the rural contracts from its scope.[38]

216. Article 3 of Law-Decree 14,384 excludes some contracts from the scope of this law, albeit they refer to the lease of property destined for agriculture, livestock or both, and are located in rural areas:

(a) The shepherding agreements of a term of utmost one year, as long as they do not renew or extend for a period which, added to the first term, results in a period longer than a year.
(b) The accidental contracts for only one harvest, which are the contracts that give the lessee the right to do up to two cultivations in one agricultural year, and due to which the lessee pays the use and enjoyment of the property with a percentage of the harvest obtained.
(c) The contracts by which land is given to the lessee to work in the improvement of the pastures, sowing of leguminous, and other crops similar, which improve the soil quality, as well as for the making of seedbeds.
(d) The contract of cattle capitalization, by which the owner of a property receives livestock from third parties, administers them and distributes the profits.
(e) The contracts of rural use executed as a civil society, in which the owner contributes to the use and enjoyment of the land.
(f) The contracts of afforestation in forestland, in which the owner of the land gives the use and enjoyment of the land.

217. In relation to the price, the parties can agree to the amount of the rent freely. The only limit refers to the subcontract, in which rent can never be higher than the one of the contract. The price can be agreed in money or in fruits or products of the land, and also the way of adjusting the price is free (Article 3 of Law 16,223). If the parties do not agree regarding the adjustment of the price, Articles 19 to 23 of Law-Decree 14,384 will apply. Article 19 refers to the revision of the contract and states that every two years, the parties can ask for a judicial revision of the price of the lease. If the revision determines that the rent must be increased by more than 30%, the lessee will have the right to terminate the contract without liability (Article 22 of Law-Decree 14,384).

218. Regarding the possibility to subcontract, in here as well as in the UCC, the subcontract is allowed unless the parties agree to the contrary. But in Article 5 of Law-Decree 14,384, it is established that the sublease cannot be registered if the lessor does not authorize the possibility to sublease in the contract.

38. Venturini Beatriz, Feuer Sofía, and others, "Manual de Contratos I," *supra*, pp. 523–524.

C. Term of the Contract

219. Regarding the term of the contract, Law 16,223 abrogated the terms established by Law-Decree 18,384, which, the same as Law-Decree 14,219, established minimum periods and extensions. Since the enactment of Law 16,223, there has been no minimum legal stability, with the only exception of the rural land destined for dairy production, which has a minimum term of four years when the lessee complied with his obligations. Regarding the maximum period for the lease, Law 16,223 states that the parties can fix the term they want, within the limits of Article 1782 of the UCC (which states as maximum limit, the period of fifteen years, except some exceptional cases in which the properties are destined to collect water, produce energy or afforestation, among others, in which the maximum period will be of thirty years).

D. Form and Registration

220. Article 4 of the Law-Decree establishes that the contract of rural lease must be in public or private deed. It also states that this contract must be registered in the General Register of Leases and Antichresis. Article 7 of Law 16,223 states that this obligation burdens the lessee. Scholars agree that this is not a solemnity requirement, and therefore, its noncompliance will not carry the nullity of the lease. But Article 6 of the Law-Decree establishes that the registration will be necessary for the performing of any paperwork before the Government offices. This will be required for the lessor as well as for the lessee, and for administrative as well as jurisdictional paperwork.

E. Statute of Limitations

221. Numeral 2° of Article 1222 of the UCC establishes a short statute of limitations of four years regarding the duty to pay the rent (in the urban leases, as well as in the rural ones).

F. Extinction

222. The causes for the extinction of this contract are the same as in the urban lease.

§4. EMPHYTEUSIS AND RENT CHARGE

I. Ground Rents: Concept and Classes

223. Ground rents, which are not common in Uruguay, can be understood as the contract that in Uruguayan law is called Censo.

224. According to Article 1856 of the UCC, a ground rent is constituted when a person contracts the obligation to pay another an annual return, in exchange of the possession of a capital or estate. This return is called ground rent (censo) or fee. The person who owes the ground rent is called censuario, and its creditor censualista (Article 1856 of the UCC).

II. Setting-Up and Characters

225. The ground rent can be constituted by will, donation, sale or any other way equivalent to the aforesaid (Article 1857 of the UCC). A ground rent can only be constituted over urban or rural properties, and it must include the land (Article 1858 of the UCC). The price must always refer to or be estimated in money. Without this requirement, the ground rent cannot be constituted (Article 1859 of the UCC). Therefore, it will not be possible for the ground rent to be paid with fruits. The non-compliance of this rule will generate the nullity of the ground rent (Article 1861 of the UCC).

226. The constitution of a ground rent must always be documented in a public deed, and registered in the respective Registry. Without this requirement, the constitution of the ground rent will not be valid, but the party who is bound to pay the ground rent will still be obliged in terms of the will or contract, and the obligation will be a personal one (Article 1860 of the UCC).

227. Every ground rent, even when constituted as perpetual, is redeemable. But the parties can agree that the termination of the ground rent will not be verified before a term that cannot exceed ten years, or without having given notice to the censualista (creditor of the ground rent), in a determined period. If the parties agree that the censuario (who owes the ground rent) can be free from the contract only after a period of more than ten years, the agreed term will be reduced to ten years (Article 1862 of the UCC).

228. It is not valid for the parties to establish, in the creation of the ground rent the prohibition of selling the property subject to ground rent, or other that imposes the censuario (who owes the ground rent) more obligations than the ones established in the UCC.

229. The obligation to pay the ground rent follows always the dominium of the estate subject to ground rent, even regarding the rent accrued before the acquisition of the estate; without prejudice to the right of the censualista to claim from the censuario that defaulted, even when he stops possessing the estate, and without prejudice of the possibility of the new possessor of the estate, to claim against the censuario or censualista a compensation (Article 1866 of the UCC).

230. The censuario is not obliged to the payment of the ground rent accrued before the acquisition of the estate subject to ground rent. But after acquiring the estate subject to ground rent, he will warrant the payment of this rent with all his estate (Article 1867 of the UCC).

231. The censuario will have the obligation to pay the ground rent, even if the estate had lost a great part of its value, or if it had become totally unprofitable. But the censuario will free from his obligation ("redemption") by placing at the disposition of the censualista the estate subject to ground rent, and paying the ground rent due, according to what is established in Article 1867 of the UCC. Nevertheless, if due to gross negligence or willful misconduct of the censuario the estate perished or became unprofitable, then he will be liable for the damages caused (Article 1868 of the UCC).

232. If the estate subject to ground rent is divided due to inheritance into smaller estates, the ground rent will be divided proportionally. To determine the value of the ground rent in each of these smaller estates, they will be valued and this valuation will be approved by the judge, in a hearing where the censualista will participate.

233. After this, the judge will order to register, at the expense of each new censuario, the ruling that establishes the portion of capital that will levy each estate. If this ruling is not registered, the censuarios will be liable for the total amount of the ground rent (before the estate was divided). If from the division, it turns out that one estate owes a ground rent of an amount lower than 500 Readjustable Units (approximately USD 15,477), the ground rent will not be divided, and each of the divided estate will be responsible for all of it (Article 1869 of the UCC). The amount imposed on one estate can be reduced or transferred to another estate. But this can be rejected by the receiving estate, when the total encumbrance after receiving the transferred part exceeds half of the value of the estate. For the calculation of the total amount of the encumbrance, other encumbrances different from the ground rent will also be taken into account (Article 1870 of the UCC).

III. Extinction

234. Redemption: The censuario can free from his obligation ("redemption") by paying the censualista or consigning the capital and ground rent due, if any. The declaration of the termination of the ground rent will be registered. If the parties do not agree otherwise, the termination cannot be done in parts (Articles 1871 and 1872 of the UCC).

235. Insolvency or Bankruptcy: The censualista cannot force the censuario to terminate the ground rent, or to deliver the capital of the ground rent, unless the censuario becomes insolvent or bankrupt, or if he does not pay the ground rent during three consecutive periods, and being judicially required to comply, did not pay in the following ten days from the requirement (Article 1873 of the UCC).

236. Destruction of the Estate: The ground rent perishes in case of the complete destruction of the estate subject to it, understanding as complete destruction, the one that makes the land disappear. In case the land reappeared, even in part, the ground rent will become in force again, but the censuario will not owe the ground rent accrued in the time in between (Article 1874 of the UCC).

237. Prescription: The statute of limitations for the payment of the rent is of thirty years starting from the date in which the censuario stopped paying the ground rent. After passing this period of time, the censualista cannot claim the accrued ground rent nor the ground rent capital (Article 1865 of the UCC).

§5. Use and Habitation/Occupation

I. Concept, Statutory Provisions, and General Features

238. The rights of use and habitation are regulated by Articles 541–549 of the UCC. The rights of use and habitation are determined by the parties in the constitutive title, receiving more or less content, in accordance with its dispositions. If the title does not establish the content of these rights, it will be understood that they will have the content set forth by Articles 545–549 of the UCC.

239. Some rules of the UCC referred to usufruct are also applicable to these real rights, such as those referred to the way these rights come into existence and expire (Article 542 of the UCC).

240. The right of use, according to Article 541 of the UCC, is a real right that consists in using a thing of another person or having the right to a portion of the fruits it produces; while the right of habitation is also a real right that consists in living free of charge in the house of another.

241. Neither the user nor the inhabitant will be required to give a deposit in order to use these rights. Notwithstanding this, the inhabitant must make an inventory, and the user has also this obligation in case the use is constituted over things that must be returned in kind (Article 543 of the UCC).

242. The use and habitation are limited to the personal necessities of the user or inhabitant and their families. The family comprises the spouse, the legitimate and natural children, acknowledged or declared so, that exist at the time of constituting the right, as well as the ones that supervene afterward. It also comprises the number of servants required by the family, and the persons that at the time of constituting the real right lived with the inhabitant or user, at their expense, and those to which the inhabitant or user owes alimony (Article 545 of the UCC).

243. Regarding the personal needs, the UCC excludes from them the ones which refer to the industry or commerce of the user or inhabitant. Therefore, the user of animals cannot employ them in the transport of the objects he trades, nor the inhabitant can use the property as a store or grocery store. It is excluded from this rule the cases in which the thing over which the right is constituted, due to its nature and ordinary use, and due to its relationship with the profession or industry of the user or inhabitant, seems destined for this use (Article 546 of the UCC).

244. The user of an estate has only the right to use objects of it for food and fuel. He must receive them from the owner or take them with his permission (Article 547 of the UCC).

245. The user and the inhabitant must use the objects over which they have a right of use or habitation, with the moderation and care of a good family father, and they must contribute to the ordinary expenses for the conservation and farming, on a pro rata basis regarding the benefit they receive from them (Article 548 of the UCC).

246. The right of use and habitation cannot be transferred to the heirs, and cannot be relinquished in any way, nor can they be loaned or rented (Article 549 of the UCC). These rights cannot be seized (Article 2363.8), and neither the user nor the inhabitant can rent, loan, or transfer any object of the things over which they have a real right of use or habitation. But they can give to others the fruits that they are allowed to consume to satisfy their personal needs (Article 549 of the UCC).

II. Extinction

247. The real rights of use and habitation will terminate for the same causes as the usufruct (*see* paragraph 163).

§6. Easements and Profits

I. Concept, Classes, and Features

248. Easements are regulated in Articles 550–611 of the UCC. The easement is an encumbrance imposed on an estate, in benefit of a different estate with a different owner. The estate that suffers the encumbrance is called servient estate, and the one that obtains a benefit is called dominant estate. The easement on the dominant estate is called active easement, and regarding the servient estate, passive easement (Article 550 of the UCC).

249. Easements can also be continuous or discontinuous. The first are those, which use can be or is incessant, without the need of an act of men, such as the light easements. The discontinuous easements are the ones that suppose an act of men, such as the easement for transit (Article 551).

250. Easements are divided also into those which are apparent because they are announced by external signs made for their use and enjoyment, such as a door, a window, and a riverbed. The nonapparent easements are those that do not show external signs of their existence, such as the easement that forbids building in certain place, or forbids building more than a certain number of floors (Article 552 of the UCC).

251. Easements cannot be separated from the estate to which actively or passively they belong.

252. Easements are indivisible. If the servient estate is divided, the easement does not vary, and the part of the estate burdened by the easement will have to suffer it. If the dominant estate is divided, all of the new owners of it will have the right to benefit from it, but without increasing the burden of the servient estate. Therefore, the new owners of the dominant estate that benefit from a transit easement, cannot demand that the direction, form, quality or width of the road be altered (Article 554 of the UCC).

253. The UCC regulates different kinds of legal easements: the right of way (Articles 581–588 of the UCC), easements of demarcation, closure and common wall (Articles 589–611), regarding the distance and intermediate works that must be done for certain constructions and plantations (Articles 612–615 of the UCC), regarding the prohibition to make windows in the common walls or in walls in certain cases, without the permission of the neighbor (Articles 616–618 of the UCC), drainage easements (Article 619 of the UCC) and regarding the duty to demolish a building or remove a tree which threatens to collapse (Article 620 of the UCC).

254. The water easements were regulated by the UCC as a legal easement, but are now regulated by the Code of Waters (Act 14859), which abrogated all the articles of the UCC referred to water easements.

II. Subjects and Object

255. The owner of an estate can constitute in his estate the easements he deems appropriate and can acquire them over the neighboring estates, with the agreement of the parties involved, and as long as they do not harm the public order, or go against the law (Article 621 of the UCC).

256. He, who constitutes the easement, must have the free administration of his peculium. Notwithstanding this, in order to constitute an easement by will, it is enough that the owner has the age at which the power to make a will is acquired (14 years for men, and 12 for women) (Article 622 of the UCC).

257. If the owner of the servient estate has only the bare property of it, he cannot constitute an easement, without the permission of the usufructuary (Article 623 of the UCC).

258. Those who have an ownership subject to condition or similar can grant an easement, but the existence of this right will be subject to the existence of the right of the owner (Article 624 of the UCC).

259. The owner of an estate with a mortgage can constitute an easement, but if this reduces the value of the property, in a way that harms the creditor, the creditor will have the right to sell the property without the easement (Article 626 of the UCC).

260. The owner of the servient estate can vary the easement with another of the same kind, or of other kind, as long as this does not affect the right of the owner of the dominant estate (Article 627 of the UCC).

261. The co-owner of an estate cannot establish an easement, without the consent of the other co-owners (Article 628 of the UCC).

262. Regarding the persons that can be benefited by the easement, and due to the fact that the easement is granted to the estate, and not to the person who owns it, the easement can be acquired by the possessors of the estate, notwithstanding if they are of good or bad faith. It can also be acquired by those who do not have the free administration of their peculium, and those that administer the estate of others in their benefit (Article 629 of the UCC). The easement can also be acquired by someone who plans to buy an estate, but the existence of this easement would depend on the purchase of the estate (Article 630).

III. Creation

263. Easements can be created by law or by an agreement of the owners (Article 555 of the UCC). The legal easements seek to provide the usefulness of the public in general, or of a village, or of certain particular persons (Article 556 of the UCC).

264. The legal easements that seek to benefit certain persons can be abrogated or modified by them.

265. The easements which are continuous and apparent at the same time can be constituted in virtue of an agreement between the parties involved, by will or through an acquisitive prescription (Article 632 of the UCC), while the discontinuous easements and those continuous but not apparent can only be constituted in virtue of the agreement between the parties involved, or by will (Article 633 of the UCC). In these cases, its possession, for a long time, is not enough to constitute them. But they can be constituted if the owner of the servient estate acknowledges the existence of this easement (Article 634 of the UCC).

266. If the owner of two estates constitutes an apparent easement between both, this is considered as a title for the easement to continue actively and passively for the future owners, unless at the time of the transfer of the property, it is established otherwise by the parties (Article 635 of the UCC).

267. If the parties agree to constitute an easement, the right to it will not be acquired until the party benefited by the easement uses it (Article 635 of the UCC). In those constituted by will, the right will be acquired at the moment of the death of the testator, without the need of using the right.

268. When an easement is constituted, it is understood that all the rights necessary for its use are also granted. This way if a person allows his neighbor to take water from a fountain located in his estate, then he allows him to walk through it in order to get to the fountain, even though this was not established in the agreement (Article 637 of the UCC).

IV. Extinction

269. Causes for extinction are provided by Article 643 of the UCC. These causes are the consolidation (when the owner of the servient estate becomes the owner of the dominant estate, or vice versa); the holder's renouncement; if the existence of the easement was subject to a condition, when the condition happens; due to the lack of use during ten years and when the state of the premises does not allow the easements to be used (but if the condition of the premises changes, allowing to use the easement again, the easement will come into force again—as long as ten years have not passed without using the easement).

§7. Licenses

270. In Uruguay, when a person inhabits free of charge the property of another person, without a contract and due to the ignorance or mere tolerance of the owner, then he is a precarious occupant.

271. This also applies to the person who remains in possession of a property after the term agreed with the owner has expired (e.g., in the case of a lease).

272. The condition of precariousness is not a right, and it does not entail a burden for the property. Moreover, it may not even be asserted against the current owner, as is shown by the fact that Article 36 of Law-Decree 14,219 (in case of urban property) as well as Article 41 of Law-Decree 14,384 (in case of rural property) state that the eviction of the precarious occupant will be done within a fifteen or thirty days' notice, instead of the one-year notice of the lessee.

§8. Restrictive Covenants

273. In Uruguay, obligations are divided into obligations of giving, doing or not doing (Article 1245 of the UCC). According to Article 1338 of the UCC, the obligations of doing or not doing, in case of breach, grant the creditor the right to a compensation. Additionally, the creditor will have the right to demand the destruction of what was done contravening what was agreed between the parties, and can obtain a judicial authorization for its destruction at the expense of the debtor.

274. One restrictive covenant would be the one that establishes an easement when it forbids the owner of an estate to build or to build beyond a definite height. In this case, the easement affects the estate, and therefore, if it is registered, it will be opposable to the new owners of it.

Chapter 5. Security Interests (*See Also* Parts II, IV and V)

275. Security interests in Uruguayan law are called derechos reales de garantía (real rights of guaranty). In Uruguay, the real rights are divided into two categories: major real rights and minor real rights. The property, which is the maximum real right, contains the powers of enjoyment and disposition. Nevertheless, over a thing owned by another person, real rights can also be established, with a limited content.

276. These minor real rights are classified, according to their function, into two categories: real rights of enjoyment (usufruct, easement, use, habitation) and real rights of guarantee (pledge and mortgage). The real rights of enjoyment grant their holder a real right of enjoyment over another person's property, while the real rights of warranty tend to secure the collection (future and possible) of a credit, through the creation of a real right over someone else's property.

277. Article 472 of the UCC states that a "Real right is the one that we have in a thing, or against a thing, without regards to a specific person. The right in a thing implies the dominium or the dismemberment of the dominium. The right against the thing can be constituted merely for guarantee; as it happens with the pledge and mortgage. From the real rights the actions of the same class are born."

278. If the debtor breaches its obligation, the creditor holder of a security interest can ask for the sale of the property (which can be owned by the debtor or by a third party) and with the money collected in the auction, the creditor can collect its debt.

279. The UCC regulates the pledge in Articles 2292–2321 and the mortgage in Articles 2322 to 2348. Meanwhile, the pledge without displacement is regulated in Law 17,228, enacted on January 24, 2001.

280. In Uruguay, the contracts are titles which do not generate a real effect, but only an obligational one (the right to have the thing). In order for the real effect to occur (and the obligation to materialize), a mode is required. Therefore, the transfer of the property (which is a real effect) does not occur with the title (i.e., purchase contract), but when, to this title, the mode is added. And the same happens with the guarantee contracts, in which a real right is not transferred (the property), but a real right is constituted (the pledge or the mortgage).

281. The creation of the real right demands publicity because the real right is absolute, i.e., opposable to third parties. This publicity is obtained, in the common pledge, with the delivery of the thing subject to pledge, to the creditor. Meanwhile, in the pledge without displacement and in the mortgage, this publicity is obtained with its registration. In all these cases, the real right does not arise until the publicity requirement is fulfilled. Therefore, this publicity is called constitutive publicity, as opposed to the declarative one.

282. The mortgage has a solemnity requirement, in virtue of which the mortgage, to be valid, has to be executed in a public deed. From the contract arises obligations, and the facultative right to register. The registration is the act that constitutes the real right of mortgage. The registration is the mode.

283. The pledge without displacement also needs to be registered in order to exist. In this case, the publicity is, at the same time, a constitutive requirement of the contract, and of the real right, which arises, simultaneously, from the registration.

284. Something alike happens in the common pledge, in which for it to exist, the contract as well as the delivery must be executed.

285. The function of guarantee, common in both contracts, gives them accessory nature. This is why the pledge and the mortgage require a principal obligation which compliance they guarantee. Both the pledge and the mortgage confer the holder the possibility to start an executory proceeding. The real guarantees only increase the possibility of the holder to collect his debt. The right to ask the judge to sell someone else's property does not arise from the guarantee, but from the unsatisfied credit.

286. It is also not possible for the creditor to appropriate these goods directly. The property subject to a real right must be auctioned, and the creditor must collect his debt from the money obtained in the auction.[39]

39. Gamarra, Jorge, "Tratado de Derecho Civil Uruguayo," Tomo 2, Third Edition, Montevideo, 1989, pp. 25 and ss.

Chapter 6. Joint Ownership

§1. Joint Ownership of Immovable Property

I. In General

287. The plural ownership of a thing by different individuals, when it occurs simultaneously, produces the phenomenon of joint ownership.

288. Joint ownership as a real right is a direct and immediate bond of the thing with the individuals. Joint ownership is a state of the property, in which the thing at the same time totally and in every part belongs currently and definitely to all the joint owners. Joint ownership, in virtue of Articles 1115 and 1151 (referred to the right of the coheirs to ask for the partition of the property inherited) is destined to go back to property through partition.[40]

289. The UCC does not regulate joint ownership but refers to it in several articles. Indeed, Article 399 refers to the partition of things that a minor co-owns with others; Article 645 refers to the interruption of the statute of limitations, when one of the co-owners uses an easement; Article 677 refers to the possibility of one co-owner to vindicate a quota of a thing co-owned and Article 1956 refers to the *pro indiviso* ownership of a thing by two spouses.

290. The co-ownership can refer to movable or immovable things, as well as to other real rights different from property.

291. The co-ownership can arise from a legal provision or by a contract between parties. An example of a legal co-ownership is the case in which the heirs inherit a property. Until the partition of such property, all of them are co-owners of it. The contractual origin could refer to the case in which two persons buy jointly a property.

292. Co-owners will have to agree to the way in which they will share the property. They will also have to pay the expenses for the maintenance of the thing subject to property, in proportion to the quota of each one, and in proportion to the use they give to it. The co-owners cannot modify the property, without the previous permission of the other co-owners. Co-owners will be free to transfer their quota of property, unless agreed otherwise. The co-ownership will terminate for the same causes as the property, and also in case the co-owners decide to divide the property.

40. Achaval, Estefania and others, "Algunas Reflexiones sobre el Régimen de la Propiedad Horizontal en el Derecho Positivo Uruguayo," published in CADE, Tomo 87, 2005.

II. Co-ownership Applied to Apartment Buildings

A. Joint Ownership of Blocks of Flats

293. The joint ownership of blocks of flats (which in Spanish Law is known as "Horizontal Property") constitutes a special kind of property that comprises a mixed object: (a) on the one side, the so-called private or individual elements, that is to say, each and every one of the flats and premises of the block, in which it is possible to separate use and enjoyment, and that have their own exit to a common element of the building or to the street; and (b) on the other side, a quota in the so-called common elements of the building (e.g., stairs, corridors, beams, walls, fronts, terraces, yards, conductions, drainages).

294. Article 748 of the UCC states that the right of property comprehends not only the ground but also, by accession, all of which is over the ground and what is beneath it. It also states that the owner can make all the plantations and constructions he deems convenient, except the ones forbidden by law or agreement. He can also make underground all the excavations and constructions he wants, and take from these excavations all the products he can get, except in case it is forbidden by law or regulations related to mines or police.

295. With the appearance of Law 10.751, some public order rules emerged, which stated that the right to enjoy and dispose of an immovable thing would have a different content. This way, the owner cannot enjoy and dispose arbitrarily of the thing, according to Article 9 of this law, because his property right is limited. Therefore, in the horizontal property, the right to enjoy and dispose of the thing is not as wide as in the right of property of the UCC. The owner has a property locked in the horizontal as well as in the vertical space.

296. The law did not create a new property right but created a new form of property. The law states that each holder of the dominium can sell or constitute real or personal rights over his portion of the thing, without the need of approval of the other co-owners. All the co-owners will have to attend to the expenses referred to common facilities.

297. Law 10.751 allows the construction or incorporation of buildings to the horizontal property regime, when they have a horizontal division blueprint, registered in the General Land Registry Office, as well as the municipal authorization and the fire insurance hired.

298. There are some exceptions to this regime, such as Chapters I and II of Law-Decree 14.261, which allow the incorporation of some buildings, without municipal authorization. In this case, co-ownership regulations are required, in which the reciprocal mortgage of the building units is provided. Also, Chapter III of Law 14.261 and Law 16.760 allowed the existence as an independent legal thing of physically non-existing units, liable to be sold or mortgaged in order to facilitate the financing of the construction of the building.

299. In 1976, Law-Decree 14,560 varied the quorum needed for the owner's assembly (Article 16), and it established that the credit for common expenses became an executory title. In 1978, Law-Decree 14,804 established rules for the formation and functioning of the civil companies destined for the construction of buildings under the horizontal property regime. In 1993 Law-Decree 15,460 was enacted, and also referred to the operation of these companies.

300. This system of horizontal property was created as an attempt to solve the need for housing for middle class that existed at that time. Although at that time there were other ways to co-own a building such as the cooperative regime, or the civil companies, this regime, unlike the others which provided only the use and enjoyment of the property, gives the co-owners an exclusive right over their property, and a co-ownership of the common goods.

301. Afterward, Law 18.795 created a new system in Articles 18 and 19, stating that buildings, which cannot be regulated by the horizontal property regime, are considered now under this regime, as long as they comply with the following requirements: (I) construction permit approved by the Municipality and (II) horizontal division project blueprints registered in the National Land Property Office. The building must be liable to be inhabited, which will be verified through a certificate signed by the Architect Director of the construction and by the Surveyor Engineer in charge, who will have to confirm certain facts (such as the fact that the constructions made coincide with the construction permit approved). A fire insurance must also be hired. After complying with these requirements, the construction becomes regulated by the horizontal property regime, without the need of the final municipal authorization. This law enacted in September 2011 was afterward regulated by Decree 97/2012. Although Law 18.795 was enacted in order to attend social housing needs, this law applies to any building already constructed.[41]

B. Private Building Complexes

302. After Law 10.751 was enacted, Parliament enacted Law 17.292 in order to include under the regime of horizontal property the private building complexes (Urbanizaciones).

303. Article 48 of this law states that the urbanizations developed in an urban or suburban area, that fall under the provisions of this law, and of the departmental regulations of territorial ordination, can be regulated under the regime of horizontal property. This law defines as "Horizontal Property Urbanization" a group of plots subject to individual property and complemented by an infrastructure of immovable goods and common services, subject to joint ownership and coadministration by the owners of the individual plots.

---

41. De los Santos, Maria Laura, "Nuevo Regimen de Incorporacion a Propiedad Horizontal," published at http://www.guyer.com.uy/wp-content/uploads/2012/12/16_Propiedad-Horizontal_LSC_06_12_2012.pdf.

304. It also establishes that when the municipal authority approves these urbanizations in rural zones, then the primitive property can be categorized as urban or suburban. These urbanizations must allow free circulation in the public streets and free accessibility to the public areas.

305. Each of the owners of a plot will be co-owner of the goods destined for a common use (Article 50 of Law 17,292). The quota for the payment of the common goods will be proportional to the area occupied by each plot, unless established otherwise in the co-ownership regulations.

§2. Joint Ownership of Movable Property

306. The rules regarding co-ownership of immovable things apply to movable things as well. Therefore, for this section what was explained in paragraphs 287–292 will be applicable.

Chapter 7. Neighborhood and Urban Problems

307. In Uruguay, the rules referred to the relationship between neighbors can be found in different statutes.

308. These rules limit the property and other real rights, in order to avoid conflicts between neighbors.

309. The UCC regulates the relationship between neighbors when it refers to the common walls, and to easements. Indeed, Article 581 of the UCC states that the owner of a property which does not have an access to the street or public road can demand the neighboring properties this access, paying the value of the land necessary for this access, and compensating any other damages it causes.

310. In reference to the common wall, Article 597 of the UCC states that the neighbor who does not want to contribute to the expenses of the common wall can free from them by giving away half of the space in which the wall or fence must be built, and renouncing to the right to the common wall or fence. Articles 598–611 also refer to the relationship between neighbors regarding common walls or fences.

311. Articles 616–618 of the UCC refer to the lights and views in the neighbor wall. Article 616 states that it is forbidden to open a window in a common wall, without the consent of the co-owner. Article 617 allows the owner of a dividing wall, which is not a common wall, to open windows, as long as they are covered with iron rods or a wire net, and is at least 3 meters from the ground of the place to be lightened up. It is also forbidden to open a window or a balcony that has a view to the rooms or yards of the neighboring property, unless there is a distance of 3 meters between both.

312. Regarding pluvial waters, Article 619 of the UCC states that there is no easement of pluvial waters, and therefore, each owner must dispose of in the roofs of their buildings, in a way that pluvial waters fall within their land with or without an access to the street, and they cannot make them fall in the neighbor's property, without his consent.

313. Another law that refers to the relationship between neighbors is Law 17,852, which refers to acoustic contamination. The prohibition to make annoying sounds is very old. In Greece, six hundred years before Christ, the artisans who worked with hammers were forced to work outside the walls of the city, in order to avoid discomfort to the inhabitants.[42] This law forbids to emit sounds above the limits established by the Ministry of Housing, Territorial Ordinance and Environment.

314. Other limitations are regulated in the laws referred to horizontal property. Article 9 of Law 10,751 states that the owners, lessees and any other person to

42. Gutierrez, Nestor, "Protección Legal contra el Ruido y la Contaminación Acústica," published in CADE 443, 2010, Montevideo.

which the owner allows to use the property, will use the apartment in a neat way, and that they cannot, among others, realize any act that disturbs the peace of the other owners, or compromises its security.

315. In case of noncompliance, the judge after receiving a claim can impose a fine that can be of between 0.5% and 20% of the cadastral value of the apartment. And in case of reoccurrence, the owner can even be forced to leave the apartment.

Chapter 8. Agrarian Problems

316. Agricultural immovables are defined in Article 283 of the Uruguayan Rural Code (Act 10.024), which defines a "Rural Establishment" in the following way: "to the effects of this Code, it is understood as a rural establishment, any real estate property that, located outside the common land, and in lack of this, outside the suburbs of the cities, villages or villas, is destined or can be destined to the raise, improvement or fattening of cattle, or to farming."

317. According to Article 31 of Act 18.308, rural land will comprise the areas of territory that the territorial ordination instruments establish as rural, including the subcategories of rural productive and rural natural, defined in Part I, Chapter 2, §2, IV.

318. Currently, trading agricultural immovable in the market is subject to limitations, established in Article 35 of Law 11.029, which introduces pre-emption rights in favor of the National Colonization Institute. This article establishes the obligation of a rural landowner, of land above 500 hectares, to offer the land to the National Colonization Institute (INC), before selling it to a third party, granting it a right of first refusal, under the same terms and price offered to a third party. This right of first refusal has already been explained in Part I, Chapter 2, §2, IV.

Part II. Movable Property and Personal Property: Chattels

Chapter 1. General Classification

319. The Civil Code divides things into corporal and incorporeal. Indeed, as was already mentioned in paragraphs 110–117 among corporeal things, the Code distinguishes between movable (muebles) and immovable (inmuebles) property, the criteria being whether they can be displaced/transported or not. They are regulated by the UCC in Articles 461–470.

320. Uruguay's Civil Code in Article 463 states that immovables are the things that cannot be transported from one place to another, such as land, mines and buildings. Article 464 states that trees and plants are also considered immovables, as long as they are fixed to the land through their roots. The fruits of the plants and trees will also be considered immovables, and will belong to the owner of the land.

321. Article 465 states that the things destined for the use, farming and benefit of an immovable will also be considered immovable, such as linings, water pipes, animals destined to help in a farm, compost, and machines destined to be used for farming.

322. However, according to Article 466, the products of the immovables, and the things accessory to them, such as herbs, wood and fruits, soil or sand, metals of a mine or the stones of a quarry, are considered movables, even before their separation, in order to establish a right in favor of the other person different from the owner.

323. Regarding the things attached to the walls, Article 467 of the UCC states that the things that provide comfort or beautification, and that are attached to the walls, if they can be removed easily, are considered movables. But, if the paintings or mirrors are attached to the walls, in a way that they become a part of them, they are considered part of the building, even if they can be separated from the walls without damaging them. The same is applicable to statues which are placed in a niche build for this purpose in the wall.

324. Regarding things which are accessories to real estate, Article 468 of the Civil Code determines that they will not cease to be part of such real estate if they are separated momentarily from it, but they will cease to be part of them if they are separated with the purpose of giving them a different destiny.

325. After distinguishing between movable and unmovable property, the Code refers to incorporeal things, and states that they can be personal (when they can be claimed by other persons) or real rights (when we have the right regarding a thing or against a thing).

§1. Tangible Movable Property and Choses in Possession

326. Tangible goods are those goods that can be physically apprehended. These goods are divided in Article 470 of the UCC into fungible and non-fungible goods.

327. Fungible goods are those that cannot be used according to their nature, without being consumed. Money is an example of a fungible good. Non-fungible goods, on the contrary, would be those that are not consumed with their normal use.

328. Fungible goods are goods that belong to a class, and that therefore are replaceable, while non-fungible goods are specific goods, unreplaceable.

329. Even though in principle fungible goods refer to movable goods only, there can also be fungible immovable goods, for example, in the case of division of plots.[43]

§2. Intangible Movable Property and Choses in Action

330. Article 471 of the UCC divides intangible movable property (incorporeal things) into real and personal rights. Real rights are the ones we have regarding a thing, or against it, without relating to a specific person. The right in the thing supposes the dominium or a dismemberment of it. The right against the thing can be constituted merely by a guarantee, as it happens in the pledge and mortgage (Article 472 of the UCC).

331. Personal rights are the ones that can be claimed from certain persons that, due to an act or due to a law, have contracted obligations, such as in the case of the money borrower. From the real rights, the real actions arise, and from the personal rights, the personal actions arise.

332. Special laws regulate some personal rights, such as the law on Intellectual Property (Law 9,739), Law on Patents (Law 17,164) and the Law on Trademarks (Law 17,011).

---

43. Yglesias, Arturo, "Derecho de las Cosas," Tomo I, Editorial FCU, Montevideo, 1997, p. 63.

§3. FUNDS (CAPITAL; INVESTMENT FUND)

333. The securities are documents that contain rights. When the document is created, the right is created as well. Securities were created as a mechanism that allowed to establish in a document a right that afterward became independent from a primitive agreement, and therefore easier to be transferred.[44]

334. In Uruguay, there are four types of securities: those securities that have as their purpose a money obligation, those that represent merchandise, the participation securities and the public securities.[45]

335. The securities that have as their purpose a money obligation include all the documents in which an obligation to give an amount of money is established: promissory notes, bill of exchange, checks and debentures.

336. Among the securities that represent merchandise, we can find waybills, boarding acknowledgements, certificates of deposit, pledge certificates. In the securities that represent merchandise, the papers document contractual relationships, while in the securities that have as a purpose a money obligation, there are two legal relationships which overlap.

337. The securities of participation refer to a document that represents the quota of capital contributed to the corporation and the rights of the partner. They are documents created by the company. The shareholder transfers his position with the sole transfer of the share. With the issuing of the share, the company does not create a new right, but documents the legal relationship of the shareholder with the company.

338. Finally, the public securities are issued to represent quotas of loans given by individuals to the State. Each security represents a fraction of the total loan.

339. Securities can be subject to contracts such as sales and donations, and it is also possible to constitute upon them real rights (usufruct and pledge). Securities can be divided, depending on its holder, as bearer, nominal or to the order. Nominal securities establish in the document the person who can request the payment of the security. It can be transferred, but first the debtor must be notified of the transmission of the security.

340. Bearer securities do not establish the name of the holder, and can be transferred freely. Finally, the securities to the order are those in which the amount stated there can be collected by the first drawee, or by the person that figures as the last acquirer. An example of this is the bill of exchange. The bill of exchange can be "endorsed" through a signature in the bill, which means that the drawer orders to pay the credit to the person endorsed (endorsee).

44. Rodriguez Olivera, Nuri, "Titulos Valores Ley 14,701," Editorial Acali, Montevideo, 1985, p. 19.
45. Rodriguez Olivera, Nuri, "Titulos Valores Ley 14,701," *supra*, p. 7.

341. The way to transfer participation securities has suffered changes in the last years. Before 2012, the shares of a corporation could be nominal or bearer shares, and bearer shares could be transferred freely, without any notification required. After Law 18,930, shareholders are required to notify the corporation when they transfer their shares, and the corporation must inform the Central Bank of Uruguay, which has a registry with all the holders of bearer shares. The companies that did not notify about the identity of at least 50% of its shareholders in a period of ninety days since the entrance into force of Law 19,288 (January 29, 2015) had as sanction its immediate dissolution.

§4. Chattels Personal and Chattels Real (*See Also* Part I)

342. In civil law, as well as in Common Law, a person can have the property of a land, or can have a life estate or a leasehold estate. The latter entails the right to use exclusively and enjoy the estate, but in a less extensive way than the one the owner of a land has. Due to their less permanent nature, in Common Law, leasehold estates are sometimes called "chattels real." In the civil law system of property, this term is not used.

343. Nevertheless, Uruguayan law regulates the rights a person can have regarding movable things, and regulates as well the rights a person might have regarding real estate.

344. Also, in Uruguayan law, there are contracts which can produce a real right, such as the contract of sale, in which the property right can be transferred, and other contracts, such as the contract of pledge or mortgage, by which a "minor real right" is constituted, this is, a right that affects someone else's property.

Chapter 2. Legal Interests

345. As was already mentioned, Uruguayan law does not distinguish between legal and equitable interests. Due to the influence of Roman law, the UCC divides movable goods into the right of property and the limited real rights in other person's property.

§1. Movable Property

346. Article 486 states that the domain (also called property—movable or immovable) is the right to enjoy and dispose of a thing arbitrarily, as long as it is not against the law or the rights of others, while Article 487 grants the owner all the powers over the thing, even the power to destroy it.

347. Article 32 of the Constitution states that: "The property is an inviolable right, but is subject to what is established by the laws enacted for reasons of general interest. No one can be deprived of his right to property unless in the cases of public necessity or public utility, established by a law, and receiving always from the National Treasure a just and previous compensation (…)."

348. As can be seen, neither the UCC nor the Constitution makes a distinction between movable and immovable things, when stating the right to property. Therefore, it must be understood that both kinds of things are comprised in this right.

349. The property of movable things, as well as of immovable things, can be defended by a vindication action, which can be brought by the person who understands to be the owner of the thing, against he who possesses it without a title.

350. The plaintiff must prove in the civil proceeding that he is the owner of the thing (Article 679 of the UCC).

351. If the judge rules against the defendant (current possessor of the movable thing), the defendant must return the thing in the period the judge establishes. Also, if he is a possessor with good faith (does not know that the thing belongs to somebody else), he will only have to pay the fruits received from the thing since the filing of the answer to the lawsuit. But if he is a possessor with bad faith, he will have to return all the fruits, and the fruits that the thing did not generate due to his negligence and that a good father of a family would have generated (Articles 693–695 of the UCC).

352. Nevertheless, if the current possessor of a stolen thing purchased it in the market or in a public sale, or to a person which normally sells this kind of things, the real owner cannot require the retrieval of the thing, without paying the price paid by the current possessor (Article 1213 of the UCC).

§2. Movable Limited Real Rights

353. Limited real rights can affect immovable as well as movable things. Article 472 of the Civil Code divides them into two categories: real rights in the thing (property and rights to use and enjoy the thing, such as the usufruct, the use, and the habitation rights), and real rights against the thing (mainly the guarantee rights of pledge and mortgage). Nevertheless, as was already said, the enumeration of real rights in the UCC is illustrative, and not numerous clausus (there can be more real rights).

354. Of these rights, some of them can only affect immovable things, and others can only affect movable things. Meanwhile, there are some real rights that can affect both kinds of things: (a) real rights that can only affect immovable things: building and planting rights, habitation, emphyteusis, rent charges (censo), real estate easements and mortgages; (b) real rights that can only affect movable things: the pledge, and the pledge without displacement; (c) real rights that can affect movable as well as immovable things: usufruct, use and leasing; (d) the real rights that can affect movable as well as immovable things, have a regulation that will sometimes vary, depending on the nature of the thing that the real right affects.

I. Guarantee Real Rights in Movables

355. The guarantee real rights that can affect movables are mainly the pledge and the pledge without displacement. They have differences in relation to immovable guarantee rights, especially regarding their content, creation, and publicity.

II. Movable Leases

356. The credit of use contract, also known as contract of leasing, is regulated in Uruguay by Law 16,072 of 1989, with the modifications introduced by Laws 16,205, 16,320, 16,906, and 17,296.

357. The contract of leasing is a contract by which a person (confirming party) obliges to allow the use of a thing to another person (the user) for a period of time, and the user obliges to pay for that use a price in money, payable periodically (Article 1 of Law 16,072). After the period of time agreed by the parties for the use of the thing is over, the user must choose between the payment of an amount of money for the purchase of the thing (a very small amount of money, compared to its true value), the renewal of the contract for a new period of time, and with a new price, or the return of the thing subject to leasing to the confirming party.

358. The law only allows to be confirming parties, the following: (i) the financial intermediaries; (ii) the companies that only perform financial activities, and that are authorized by the Uruguayan Central Bank for the execution of this contract;

(iii) the Retirement and Pension Fund for Notaries, the Retirement and Pension Fund for University Professionals, and the Retirement and Pension Fund for Bank employees.

359. There is also another kind of leasing called operational leasing, which includes, among the options of the user at the end of the period of the contract, to substitute the thing of the contract with another one, and establish a new price.

360. Normally, this contract is used for the purchase or for the use of industrial vehicles, machinery, and private vehicles.

361. In this contract, the confirming party acquires the thing subject to leasing. When it delivers it to the user, the confirming party does not transfer the property of the thing, so in principle it could be understood that the confirming party maintains its property.

362. Nevertheless, this right is affected by several limitations. The principal attributes of this right are transferred to the user, or are limited by law. The right of use is acquired by the user. The right to transfer the thing belongs to the confirming party, but it can only transfer the thing subject to this contract to another institution that can be a confirming party (Article 11 of Law 16,072), and, after the registration of the contract, Law 16,072 confers the user a real right that protects him from any subsequent transfer or encumbrance (Article 8 of Law 16,072).[46]

46. Rodriguez Olivera, Nuri and Lopez, Carlos, "Régimen Jurídico del Contrato de Leasing," published on http://www.derechocomercial.edu.uy/ClaseContCrUsoRegimen.htm.

Chapter 3. Equitable Interests

363. As was already mentioned in paragraph 97, in Uruguay, unlike Common Law countries, we do not differentiate between "legal interests" and "equitable interests." In Uruguay, property and minor real rights are considered legal interests, and are regulated by law.

Chapter 4. Security Interests (*See Also* Parts I, IV and V)

364. As was already pointed out in paragraph 275, security interests in Uruguayan law are called derechos reales de garantía. In Uruguay, the real rights are divided into two categories: major real rights and minor real rights. The property, which is the maximum real right, contains the powers of enjoyment and disposition. Nevertheless, over a thing owned by another person, real rights can also be established, with a limited content.

365. These minor rights are classified, according to their function, into two categories: real rights of enjoyment (usufruct, easement, use, habitation) and real rights of guarantee (pledge and mortgage). The real rights of enjoyment grant their holder a real right of enjoyment over another person's property, while the real rights of warranty tend to secure the collection (future and possible) of a credit, through the creation of a real right over someone else's property.

366. Security interests that can affect movable property are usufruct, use, pledge and mortgage.

Chapter 5. The Publicity of Movable Real Rights

§1. The Role of Possession

367. The possession of movable things and movable real rights is fundamental in order to prove the property of them. Indeed, due to the fact that, according to Article 649 of the UCC, the person who has the possession of a thing is presumed the owner of it, unless someone else proves the contrary.

368. Article 649 also grants the following rights to the person who holds the possession of a thing: (i) he can file possessive actions; (ii) when possessing peacefully and publicly for a whole year, without being interrupted, he acquires the right of possession and is excused from responding of it; (iii) he gains the right to take over the fruits of the thing until the date of the answer of the lawsuit, when he is a good faith possessor; (iv) he can prescribe the dominium and the other real rights; (v) after losing the possession, he can use the vindication action, even if he is not the owner, against the person that possesses it with a title inferior to his own.

369. In the case of immovable property, possession is not as important as in the movable things because in this case the principal publicity of the property of a thing is given by the registry of the right in the Real Estate Section of the Property Register. Notwithstanding this, there are some movable things which can also be registered in the Property Register, such as motor vehicles.

370. But in general, movable goods cannot be identified, and therefore cannot be registered. Therefore, the possession of them is the principal proof of their property. This is stated in Article 649 of the UCC.

§2. The Registry of Movable Things

371. In Uruguay, the Property Registry has a section for immovable things and one for movable things. Under the section for movable things, there are three more registers: National Register of Motor Vehicles, the National Register of Pledges without Displacement, and the National Register of Aircrafts.

372. In the National Register of Pledges, the law allows registering the contracts referred to this kind of pledge as well as the leasing contracts (Article 31 of Law 16,871).

373. Law 17,228 referred to the pledge without displacement (January 7, 2000), introduced a new real guarantee regarding movable things. As the pledge, this guarantee allows its holder to ask for the judicial auction of the thing, in case the debtor does not pay his debt on time. But in this case, the creditor will not have the possession of the things subject to pledge. This pledge was created in order to solve the problem that arose, when the debtor wanted to give as a guarantee of the payment of a debt the movable things he owned, but at the same time needed those things in order to pay the debt (such as the machinery of his work). This guarantee can only fall upon movable things and rights that can be identified (Article 3 of Law 17,228).

374. Due to the fact that the creditor would not have the possession of the things subject to pledge, the law established the obligation to register the contract of pledge without displacement in the National Register of Pledges without Displacement. The only exceptions to this rule are: (i) the pledge over motor vehicles which is registered in the National Register of Motor Vehicles; (ii) the pledge over commercial or industrial establishments, which is registered in the National Register of Commerce; (iii) the pledge over industrial property rights, which is registered in the National Office of Industrial Property; and (iv) the pledge over forests, which is registered in the General Register of Forests of the Forestry Office of the Ministry of Agriculture, Livestock and Fishing.

375. The things subject to pledge can be sold, but the delivery of them cannot be done unless the seller pays its debt to his creditor, unless the creditor consents the transfer of the property of the thing subject to pledge. In this case, the change of owner of the thing must be registered in the National Registry of Pledges without Displacement (Article 10 of Law 17,228).

376. The second paragraph of Article 3 of Law 17,228 allows the parties to establish a floating pledge, in virtue of which the parties can agree that some things that enter into the estate of the debtor are comprised in the pledge, substituting or complementing the original appointed things, and must remain in the same place as the original ones.

377. Among Uruguayan scholars, there is a discussion regarding the effect of the registration of the contract of pledge without displacement in the Register. Cacciatore, taking into account what is established in Article 7 of Law 17,228 (which states that the pledges without displacement will be on writing and will not be opposable to third parties until its registration), affirms that the publicity is declarative, and not constitutive of this right. While Gamarra affirms that, in virtue of Article 1 of Law 17,228, this kind of pledge is regulated also by the UCC, which includes the pledge among the real rights. And Article 54 of the Law of Registries states that the registration will determine the creation of the real right when the legislation in force determines it so. In this case, according to Gamarra, we would be before a mortgage over a movable thing, and according to the UCC, the registration is a requirement for the real right to be constituted (Article 2323).[47]

378. The Registry of Movable Things provides publicity of all the acts or contracts that affect the thing subject to pledge: endorsements, extensions, reregistrations, purchases and cancelations, among others (Article 31 of Law 16,871).

379. The requests of information of pledges or leasing, regarding things, are requested with the name of the giver of the pledge or user, and is requested in the

47. Gamarra, Jorge, "Tratado de Derecho Civil Uruguayo," Volume VIII, Montevideo, 2010, pp. 95–97.

Department in which the things are located, unless these things have a registration number, in which case they will be requested in the Department of the registration with this number.

380. Regarding its location, the Registry of Movable Things is in the same building as the Property National Registry. The way information is provided in both registries is the same: a specific document is assigned per item, and the information of these documents is provided through a registry certificate (certificado registral).

Part III. Acquisition of Property Rights

381. The ways to acquire real rights in Uruguayan law are established on the Third Book of the UCC, called *Of the Ways to Acquire the Dominium*. This book comprises the following ways: occupancy, accession, contracts followed by the delivery of things, inheritance (with or without will) and acquisitive prescription.

382. All of these ways allow acquiring property and limited real rights, over movable and immovable things, except for occupancy, which applies only to the acquisition of property, and only in the case of movables.

383. These ways to acquire property can also be divided depending if there was a previous owner that transferred the property or the limited right of a thing (contract and inheritance), or if there was no transfer whatsoever (occupancy, accession and acquisitive prescription).

Chapter 1. Transfer of Property by Contract *Inter Vivos*

384. One of the ways the UCC states as a way of acquiring real rights in Uruguayan law is the delivery of the things. Unlike other systems of law, such as the French, in Uruguayan law to acquire property, a title and a way are needed (acquisition is not merely consensual).

385. The title without the way produces only obligations for the parties, but does not transfer the property or limited real right. Therefore, it can be said that in Uruguay, the transfer of property (real effect) is achieved through a complex transaction that requires the juxtaposition of two transactions, of a different legal nature: (i) a binding transaction, which would be a contract, that must gather the requirements to transfer the property or limited real right; and (ii) the dispositive transaction, which would be a conveyance way.

386. The acquisition title is the contract the parties execute, and that binds them: a sale, an exchange contract, etc., while the conveyance way refers to the delivery of the thing subject to transfer.

387. The property is transferred in the moment in which the delivery is performed because this transaction is the one that has real effect (Articles 705, 758, 769 and 775 of the UCC), but the delivery of the thing by itself is not enough to generate this effect if it is not accompanied by an appropriate title, a contract which is suitable to transfer the dominium (Article 769, paragraph 3).

388. In Uruguayan law, there is a difference between the contract and the act of transference of property. Due to the fact that the contract is an obligational transaction, for the real effect to take place, the act of transfer of property (traditio, or delivery) in a moment after the execution of the contract must take place, as the compliance of the obligations agreed in it.

389. This is an important difference from the regime of the contract with real effect, which applies in the Italian and French law, in which the transfer of the real right happens at the moment of the execution of the contract, as an automatic and immediate effect. The transfer happens when the parties give their consent.[48]

390. The conveyance way, called by the Uruguayan law "tradition," is regulated by Articles 758 to 775 of the UCC. Article 758 defines the tradition as "the transfer that a person does to another, of the possession of a thing, with the power and intention of transferring the property of it."

391. In Uruguay, tradition can be real or presumptive. The real tradition is the one that happens by the corporeal apprehension of the thing, made by the purchaser

48. Gamarra, Jorge, "Tratado de Derecho Civil Uruguayo," Volume VIII, *supra*, pp. 47–48.

or other in his name. If the tradition is made regarding a real estate, then it is verified when the acquirer goes where the property is or sends a representative, in order to take possession, with the consent of the disponer ("tradente"). When the thing to be delivered is a building, the tradition happens when the disponer takes away his furniture and allows the acquirer to introduce his. If the thing to be delivered is a movable, then the tradition occurs when the thing subject to tradition is put in the hand of the acquirer, or of his representative. Finally, if the thing subject to tradition is part of a demesne ("heredad"), such as the standing trees or the rocks of a quarry, then the tradition occurs when these things are separated from the land to which they are attached, with the consent of the disponer (Articles 760–762 of the UCC).

392. The presumptive tradition or symbolic tradition is applicable when the thing is not delivered, but what is delivered is an object that represents it, and that allows its taking of possession. The symbolic tradition can take place: (i) through the delivery of the keys of the warehouse where the things to be delivered are located; (ii) through the delivery that the seller or donor of a property makes of the keys to the buyer or donee, after taking his furniture out; and (iii) through the delivery of the titles of the thing. If this is an immovable, the disponer must also leave it ready for the taking of possession of the acquirer (Articles 763 and 764 of the UCC).

393. Another symbolic tradition is the tradition through the sight, which occurs when the disponer or his representative shows the thing to the acquirer or his representative, giving him the possibility to take possession of it (Article 765 of the UCC).

394. When the acquirer already has the possession of the thing subject to sale, exchange or donation, the mere consent of the parties constitutes tradition. It also is understood as tradition: (i) the clause in which it is stated that the disponer gives the possession of the thing to the acquirer or donee; (ii) the clause in which the donor states that he withholds the usufruct of the thing subject to donation; and finally, (iii) the clause in which in a contract of sale or donation, the donor or seller leases the thing, of the buyer or donee. For these clauses to have the effect of a real tradition, it is required that they are stated in a public deed (Articles 766 and 767 of the UCC).

395. The tradition of the rights happens: (i) through the delivery of the documents that constitute the title, or (ii) through the use of the acquirer, and the patience of the disponer, such as what happens in the easements. In the case of the transfer of credits, the tradition happens when the transfer is communicated to the debtor. Nevertheless, this will not apply to the credits transferable through endorsement, or bearer credits, or others, according to specific laws (Article 768 of the UCC).

396. In order to acquire the property through tradition, it is required that the: (i) tradition is made by the owner or his representative; (ii) person making the tradition or the one consenting it is capable of transferring the property; (iii) tradition is made in virtue of a title able to transfer the property; and (iv) parties consent it. In the purchase agreement, in addition to these requirements, it is necessary that the purchaser has paid the price or has given guarantor, pledge or mortgage, or has obtained an extension for the payment (Article 769 of the UCC).

397. Therefore, for the tradition to be effective, the disponer must be the owner of the thing. Nevertheless, if the disponer is not the owner, Article 1669 of the UCC states that the purchase of a thing belonging to other is valid. Nevertheless, the real effect of transfer of the property will not occur. And the agreement, regarding the real owner, will be irrelevant because no one can transfer more rights than the ones they have, and the owner has not been a party in the agreement (Article 1293 of the UCC). Therefore, the sale of a thing belonging to other is valid and produces obligations (the seller must purchase these things in order to comply with the acquirer) but does not produce the real effect, until the seller becomes owner of the things and transfers its property to the acquirer.[49]

398. The same happens when, although the seller is the owner of the thing, the law forbids him to sell it to the other party. For example, Uruguayan law forbids a spouse to sell a property to the other spouse (Article 1675 of the UCC).

399. In the forced sales that are made in virtue of a judicial decree, after a petition of a creditor, in a public auction, the person that makes the tradition of the property is the disponer, through the judge, who is his legal representative (Article 770 of the UCC).

400. If there is an error regarding the identity of the kind of the thing to be delivered, or the person to which it must be delivered, or regarding the title, the tradition becomes invalid. But if the error refers only to the name, the tradition is valid (Article 771 of the UCC). Also, if the law requires a special solemnity (e.g., public deed), the property will not be transferred if this is missing.

49. Gamarra, Jorge, "Tratado de Derecho Civil Uruguayo," Volume VIII, *supra*, pp. 69–70.

Chapter 2. Transfer of Property by Death

401. Property and other real rights can also be acquired through inheritance, which is "the action of inheriting the deceased and representing him in all the rights and obligations that were not extinguished with death" (Article 776 of the UCC). The succession by death can be testamentary or intestate. In the testamentary succession, the deceased, while living, appoints his heirs through a unilateral act: the will. In the second case, the heirs are appointed by law. The succession of a person can be partly testamentary and partly intestate (if the will only covers part of the deceased rights and obligations) (Article 778 of the UCC).

402. The testament is an act that can be revoked at any time, by which a person disposes of all or part of his properties. Two or more people cannot share a single will (it is individual) (Article 781 of the UCC). The testator cannot appoint a representative in order to draft his will (Article 782 of the UCC). The will is formal; it must be drafted taking into account certain solemnities (with some exceptions).

403. The testator is not free to dispose of all of his properties by testament. Indeed, Uruguay's inheritance laws follow the European-Continental model (as most of Latin America does) which establishes that a great part of the deceased's assets in Uruguay will mandatorily be assigned to certain relatives ("forced heirs") if such relatives exist: generally, the person's children or descendants and in case the deceased does not have descendants, the deceased's parents or grandparents. In case the deceased has descendants, he must leave them 50% of his estate in case of having one child, two-thirds of his estate in case of having two children, and three-fourths of his estate in case of having three or more children (Article 887 of the UCC). If the testator does not have children, he must leave 50% of his estate to his parents or ascendants.

404. The widow or widower also has a right called conjugal portion. The spouse's right to a portion of the estate applies only in the case the spouse's personal assets value is inferior to a portion of the deceased's estate (considering among his or her assets, what belongs to him/her due to community property, and what was inherited from his/her spouse). The portion of the deceased estate to be compared to the spouse's assets will be determined depending on the existence of other forced heirs: if there are no children, the portion will amount to one-fourth of the estate, and if there are children, this amount will vary. If the spouse's personal assets, plus the value of half of the community property, plus the assets inherited, results in an amount inferior to the portion that would correspond to her in the deceased's estate, then the spouse will have the right to receive a complement (assets left by the deceased, that must be added in order to obtain the value of the conjugal portion). But if the spouse's assets are superior to the conjugal portion, she will not have a right to it, unless she renounces her existent assets.

405. The deceased's spouse will also have a real right of habitation regarding the property where he/she lived with the deceased. The heirs can decide to keep this property, but in this case will have to provide the spouse another property that he/she must approve. This real right is analyzed by Sonia Salgado and Andrea Tellechea in their monograph "Aportes para un Estudio de Títulos."[50] This right comprises also the right to use during his/her life, free of charge, the furniture of the property. But both rights will be lost if the spouse marries again, or lives with another person, or acquires another property, similar to the conjugal home (Article 881.3 of the UCC).

406. Finally, Article 871 of the UCC states that the alimony that the testator owes at the time of his death must be deducted from the estate of the deceased in an amount that the judge must determine. Therefore, in Uruguay, the testator can leave only part of his estate to the person he wants to appoint as heir (this portion will amount to the difference between the value of his estate and what has to be handed to his forced heirs, spouse, and alimony creditors—Article 870 of the UCC).

407. Regarding the acceptance of the inheritance, Uruguayan law establishes that the acquisition of the deceased things and rights will occur after the acceptance of the inheritance, which can be accepted without any condition, or under benefit of inventory (Article 1061 of the UCC). If the heir accepts under the benefit of inventory, he will be liable for the obligations of the deceased for the amount of the things inherited (Article 1097 of the UCC). Otherwise, he will have to respond to those obligations with his own estate as well (Article 1069 of the UCC).

408. The acceptance of the inheritance has no deadline. The heirs can accept it at any time. Nevertheless, after nine days after the death of the deceased, any interested party (e.g., creditors) can request that the heir declares if he accepts or refuses the inheritance, and in this case, the judge will give the heir a period of time that cannot exceed of forty days since receiving notice, in order to inform his decision. If this period passes without any declaration of the heir, it will be understood that he refuses the inheritance (Article 1070 of the UCC).

409. The effects of the acceptance or refusal of the inheritance will be retroactive to the time in which the succession was opened (Article 1051 of the UCC). If there is more than one heir, a joint ownership of the inheritance will come into effect, and each heir will be the owner of a quota of the things and rights left by the deceased. This quota can be transferred to third parties (Article 1120 of the UCC). For the heirs to be owners of specific things of the inheritance, the partition of the inheritance must be performed (Articles 1115–1167 of the UCC).

410. The legatees are not "universal successors" or successors of all the rights and duties of the deceased, but they only have the right to a specific thing, right or action (Article 912 of the UCC).

---

50. Salgado, Sonia and Tellechea, Andrea, "Aportes para un Estudio de Títulos," published at http://www.fder.edu.uy/material/salgado-tellechea_aportes-para-un-estudio-de-titulos.pdf. This monograph was coordinated by Dora Bagdassarian, Montevideo, p. 123.

Chapter 3. Possession

§1. Acquisitive Prescription

411. The acquisitive prescription, also called usucapion (which comes from usucapio, which means to acquire through the use), is a way of acquisition of the property or other real right, through the possession during a period of time, and with the requirements established by law.[51] For Fabbrini, usucapio meant "acquisition through possession," while usus meant possession.[52]

412. In order to acquire an immovable property or a real right through usucapion, the possession of the thing must be continuous and non-interrupted, peaceful, public, not misleading, and as an owner. We will now proceed to analyze each one of these requirements.

413. To possess in a continuous way (Articles 1188 and 1196) means that the behavior of the possessor must translate in a steady exercise of possessory acts, over the thing he is possessing. An example of the acts expected to be performed by the possessor, are established in Article 666 of the UCC,[53] which states that the possession of the land must be proven by positive acts, of the kind that only the right of property allows to do, such as the cut of wood, the construction of buildings, the construction of enclosures, the planting or sowing, and others of equal significance, which must be performed without the consent of the one challenging the possession. The continuity or discontinuity depends on the behavior of the possessor. It is not necessary to be all the time in contact with the thing, it is enough to use the thing as a normal owner, diligent and careful, would have used it.[54]

414. Meanwhile, the requirement referred to the fact that the possession cannot be interrupted, which is established in Articles 649 paragraph 3, 1196, 1212 and 1232 and et seq. of the UCC, means that the possession cannot be affected by natural, or third party acts. Article 1232 of the UCC states two kinds of interruptions: the natural and the civil interruption. In the first one, the possession ceases: (a) because it is impossible to perform acts of possession to the property—for example, in case of a flood, or (b) because it is being possessed by someone else. In the first case, the time during which the property could not be possessed cannot be counted for the prescription of the thing, while in the second case, the possessor will have to start from scratch, unless he wins over the possession again through a legal proceeding. In the second kind of interruption, this is, the civil interruption, it occurs when the possessor is served with a lawsuit. After the interruption, the possessor

51. Howard, Walter, "Modos de Adquirir," Editorial University of Montevideo, Montevideo, 2002, p. 417.
52. Fabbrini, Fabrizio, Novissimo Digesto Italiano, T. XX, Unione Tipografico—Editrice Torinese, Torino, 1982, p. 281.
53. Howard, Walter, "Modos de Adquirir," *supra*, p. 391.
54. Howard, Walter, "Modos de Adquirir," *supra*, p. 392.

starts possessing from scratch, and the time passed is not considered for the acquisition by acquisitive prescription. If the possessor acknowledges someone else as owner, this does not interrupt the usucapion, but is regulated as a renunciation to it.

415. To possess peacefully, which is stipulated by Articles 649 paragraph 3, 663, and 1196 of the UCC, means that the possession, to be able to acquire the property of a thing or right, must not be maintained through violence or force. But if the thing is obtained through violence, the possessor can equally acquire the property of the thing through usucapion. But to do this, the period of time of possession required, for the usucapion to take place, will start computing since the violence ceases.[55]

416. The public possession is required by Article 1196 of the UCC, and refers to the requirement to possess the property in a way that the ones who have the right to oppose to it can take notice of it. If after some time the possessor stops using the thing publicly, then the period of possession will disappear, and the period will start again when the possessor starts possessing the thing publicly once again.[56]

417. The not misleading possession, required by Article 1196 of the UCC, is the most discussed requirement in Uruguayan jurisprudence. The possession is not misleading, when from the behavior of the possessor it can be inferred that he wants to acquire the thing or real right through usucapion. Finally, to possess as an owner, can refer to other rights, other than property. For example, someone who wants to acquire by prescription the real right of usufruct must possess as usufructuary. This requirement is easier to prove in the abbreviated usucapion, in which the possessor has a title that gives him the right to possess that thing (but the title is not valid, and he does not know it). This requirement for Guillot[57] implies to possess as an owner, and not in the name of others. This is not a requirement of the prescription, but of the possession itself, according to Article 646. If the person does not possess as an owner, there will be no possession, but a mere tenancy of the thing.

418. In Uruguayan law, acquisitive prescription is divided between the prescription of immovables and of movables. The acquisitive prescription of immovable can be of two kinds: the one that requires ten years of possession, which is applicable to possessors with just title and good faith, whether the owner lives in the country or abroad[58]. The second kind requires a possession of twenty years, and applies when the possessor does not have just title and good faith (Articles 1204 and 1211 of the UCC[59]). If the owner gives the mere tenancy of an immovable to a person,

55. Howard, Walter, "Modos de Adquirir," *supra*, p. 395.
56. Howard, Walter, "Modos de Adquirir," *supra*, pp. 396/397.
57. Guillot, "Comentarios del Codigo Civil. De la Posesión y de la Reivindicación," p. 65, cited by Howard, Walter, *supra*, p. 402.
58. Before Jul. 24, 2020, the period of time to acquire immovables was of ten years if the owner lived in the country, and of twenty if he lived abroad. Now the period is the same in both cases (ten years), as long as the possessor proves a possession with just title and good faith.
59. This period used to be of thirty years, but was modified by Law 18.889, which came into force on Jul. 24, 2020.

and after some time, this person starts possessing it as an owner, the possessor can acquire the property of the thing in virtue of this type of prescription.

419. The good faith mentioned above consists in believing at the time of the purchase that the seller of the thing is the owner and can transfer it. The good faith is presumed, and it is enough that it existed at the time of the purchase (Article 1207 of the UCC). Just title refers to a contract that should be legal and able to transfer the property or the real right to the possessor, but it cannot due to the fact that the seller is not the real owner of the property (Article 1208 of the UCC). The current possessor can add to his possession the time that the previous possessor (believed to be the owner) possessed the thing (Article 1206).

420. For movable things, in order to acquire them through acquisitive prescription, it is required to have possessed them during three years, with just title and good faith, having been the owner in the country or abroad. If the possessor does not have just title and good faith, he must possess the thing for six years, in order to acquire it (Article 1214 of the UCC). This does not apply to the person who stole the thing, nor his accomplices.

§2. Acquisition a Non-Domino

421. Uruguayan scholars analyze two cases of acquisition a non-domino (to purchase a property from someone who is not the owner of the thing). According to Gamarra, when a person does not have legal standing to transfer the property of a thing, the property is not transferred, but when the parties sign a contract fit to transfer the property and act with good faith, possession will be transferred.[60] Also, it is important to point out that regarding the obligational transaction, the legal standing is not a requirement for efficacy, and because of this the contract will be valid and effective (it produces personal effects), even though the legal standing is lacking. This is why the sale of another person's things is valid according to the UCC (Article 1669 of the UCC). Notwithstanding this, the dispositive transaction will not produce its typical effect (real effect) if the transferor does not have the legal standing to transfer the property. But the celebration of a contract that is fit to transfer the property of a thing has importance in the field of acquisitive prescription. As was already mentioned, in this field, in order to acquire the property in the abbreviated period of ten years, it is required just title and good faith.

422. Regarding the acquisition, a non-domino of movable things, our system followed the Roman law system, which allowed to vindicate the movable thing as long as the property right of the owner had not been extinguished by acquisitive prescription of a third party. This system is different from the German system, which states that "possession is equivalent to title." This system was adopted by most countries, among others: France, Italy, Germany and Argentina. This system states

60. Gamarra, Jorge, "Tratado de Derecho Civil Uruguayo," Tomo octavo, Montevideo, p. 71.

that the owner of a thing cannot vindicate it from a person who acquired its possession with good faith. In the German system, the owner will only have a personal action against the person who breached his trust and sold the property of the movable thing to a third party.

423. Therefore, in the German system, the owner is deprived of the vindictive action, establishing an acquisition a non-domino in benefit of the third possessor with good faith. Meanwhile, in the Uruguayan system, the principle that applies is the principle of legal standing, according to which no one can transfer more rights than the ones they have. Therefore, someone who is not the owner of a thing cannot transfer its property. And therefore, if he sells this thing to a third party with good faith, the owner can file a vindictive action and recover the possession of the thing (as long as he did not lose the property of the thing through acquisitive prescription).

424. An exception of this rule is the case of erroneous registry certificates. Although it is not established in Uruguayan laws, most jurisprudence has understood that in the cases in which a person, before purchasing a thing, asks for a registry certificate, if this certificate, due to an error, throws that the current owner is the previous one (or another person different from the current owner), and the purchaser buys the thing trusting in the registry information, the third party with good faith will remain as the owner of the thing, and the real owner will have a personal action against the previous owner and against the registry, but will not be able to vindicate his property from the third party. Jurisprudence justifies this in the importance of registry information for commerce.

Another exception is the case in which a third party with good faith buys or becomes the beneficiary of a guarantee of a thing from someone who appears as the owner, after celebrating a simulation contract with the real owner.[61]

425. An example of this is the ruling 219/2001 issued by the Supreme Court on October 8, 2001.[62] In this case, the Bank was the beneficiary of a mortgage, granted by the owner of a property, which afterward turned out not to be the real owner. This happened because the real owner celebrated with him a simulation contract, in virtue of which he appeared to be the real owner when he was not. The Court understood that, even though the purchase was void, the mortgage, granted by whom was not the owner of the property, was not void. And this is so, due to the exception established in Article 1580 of the UCC, which states that the third party who acts with good faith and ignores the existence of a simulation contract cannot be harmed by this contract.

61. Tome, Miguel Angel, "Negocios Jurídicos Simulados y Fraudulentos," FCU, Montevideo, 2008, p. 158.
62. *Roca, Juan Jose v. Davyt Bouissa, Ana Elena and others*, SCJ, 219/2001 (2001).

Chapter 4. Accession

426. The term "accession" derives from the Latin word "accession," which means the increase of something. Article 731 of the UCC categorizes the accession as a way to acquire the fruits of a thing, or its incorporations, being them natural or artificial. Therefore, two kinds of accession are established: (i) the one that results from the generative energy of the things (in which the owner becomes owner of what the thing produces), and (ii) the one that results from the incorporation of a thing that does not belong to the owner, to a thing that belongs to him. The first one is called discrete accession, while the second one is called continuous accession.[63]

427. The UCC includes these categories of accession, and also states differences between movable and immovable things. Notwithstanding this, when the accession is mentioned as a way to acquire property or other limited real rights, the law is referring to the continuous accession only.

428. The UCC divides the regulation of the accession into three chapters: (i) the accession regarding the product of the things (Articles 732–735), which is the discrete accession, of fruits or production; (ii) the accession of movable things (Articles 736–747) refers to the continuous accession to this kind of things, and (iii) the one referred to immovables (Articles 448 et seq.), and is divided into: (a) artificial accession, which refers to building, sowing and plating, and is known as the accession of a movable to an immovable; and (b) natural accession, which comprises the flood, isle formation and change of riverbed, which is known as the accession of one immovable to another.[64]

§1. Immovable Accession

429. According to Article 748 of the UCC, the right of property does not limit to the surface of the land, but extends by accession to what is over the surface, and beneath it. The owner can do over the land all the plantations and constructions that he deems convenient, except those forbidden by law or due to an agreement. He can also do beneath the land all the constructions and excavations that he wants, and take from beneath all the products he can get, notwithstanding the provisions of law and regulations related to mines and police.

430. All the works, sowings and plantations made in a land are presumed to be made and paid by the owner, unless proven otherwise. If someone with good faith builds in his own land or building, with materials that belong to someone else, he will become the owner of them after incorporating them into the construction, but will be obliged to pay to the owner of the materials the fair price or to give him other materials of the same nature, quality and aptitude. But if he acted with bad faith, he will also have to pay the damages, notwithstanding the criminal liability.

63. Howard, Walter, "Modos de Adquirir," *supra*, p. 101.
64. Howard, Walter, "Modos de Adquirir," *supra*, pp. 102–103.

Nevertheless, if the owner of the materials was aware of its use, the owner of the property will only have to pay for the materials, or return some of the same quality. The same rule applies to the person who plants or sows in his own land, with vegetables or seeds which belong to somebody else (Articles 749 and 750). This is a clear application of the principle which states that the accessory follows the principal.

431. The owner of a property in which other person without his consent, builds, plants or sows will have the right to appropriate the building, plantation or sown field, but will have to compensate the person with the compensations established for the possessors of good and bad faith: if he acted with good faith, he can keep the fruits received until receiving notice of the complaint, and if he acted with bad faith, he will have to give back all the fruits received since the possession and those a good family father would have received. Alternatively, the owner can force the person who built or planted, to pay him the fair price of the land with the legal interests for all the time in which he possessed the land, and can force the person who sowed to pay him rent and compensate him for the damages suffered. If the owner was aware of the building, planting or sowing, he will be forced, in order to recover his land, to pay the price of the building, plantation or sown field.

432. Regarding the cases of natural accession, the UCC regulated these cases in Articles 752–757. These cases afterward were regulated by the Code of Waters, and the articles of the UCC were abrogated. These cases mentioned by the Code of Waters refer to situations in which a part of land from another property becomes a part of a different land, by accession, due to the action of the water. One example of natural accession is the case regulated by Article 62 of the Code of Waters, called "Alluvion." This alluvion can refer to two scenarios: (i) the growth formed successively and imperceptibly in the shore of the rivers, streams, lakes and ponds, due to the consolidation with the land of particles transported through water; and (ii) the space left by the water when it withdraws imperceptibly from the shore. In both cases, the increase of land experimented by these properties will belong to the owners of them, in proportion to their properties fronts. The persons who suffered a loss of land due to the alluvion cannot ask for a compensation to the ones who received a benefit from it. This can be justified by the fact that the flood is not caused by the will of the parties, and because it is quite impossible to determine which part of the land left which property and ended up in which other property.[65]

§2. Movable Accession

433. The UCC regulates three cases of movable accession, the "adjunction," the "specification," and the "mixture." The first case consists in the joining of two movable things, of different owners, joined in a way that they become one thing and cannot be separated without damaging them. In this case, the new thing will belong to the owner of the principal object (this article applies the principle that the accessory

65. Howard, Walter, *supra*, pp. 208–211.

follows the principal). But the owner of the principal object will have to pay to the other owner the value of the accessory thing. If the objects can be separated without harming them, they must be separated and continue belonging to their respective owners (Article 737 of the UCC). Articles 738 and 739 establish different criteria in order to define which object should be considered principal, and which one accessory. In this line of thinking, this article states that if one thing is adorned or perfected by the other, then the first one will be the principal. But if the thing that was joined to the principal is more beautiful, and it was used without the knowledge of the owner, then he can ask that the thing joined to the principal be returned to him, even if this entails causing harm to the principal thing. Finally, if it is not possible to determine which of the two things joined is the accessory, it will be considered as principal the one with a higher value, or the one bigger if they have the same or similar values.

434. The second case analyzed by the UCC is the case of "specification," which occurs when someone uses materials of another person in order to create a new thing. In this case, even if the materials can be returned to their original state, the owner of the materials has the right to claim the new thing, paying for the work done. But if the work done exceeded by far the value of the materials, the work will be considered as principal, and the artisan or artist will have the right to keep the thing, but will have to pay the value of the materials used. If the materials used belonged to the one who did the new thing and to another person, and these materials cannot be separated, without causing damage to the thing, the new thing will belong jointly to both owners, on a pro rata basis (one will own part of the value of the materials, and the value of the work done, while the other will own part of the value of the materials) (Articles 740–741 of the UCC).

435. Finally, the Code regulates a third case of movable accession called "mixture." In this case, a thing is formed due to the mixture of dry or liquid materials, belonging to different owners. If the materials can be separated without causing damage, then the owner that did not consent the mixture can ask for their separation. And if any of the materials can be considered principal regarding the other, then the owner of the principal can claim the thing resulting from the mixture, and will have to pay the other the value of his materials. But if the materials cannot be separated without damage, and none of them can be considered principal, the owners of them will acquire the joint ownership of them, on a pro rata basis, taking into account the quantity, quality and value of the materials used owned by each one (Articles 742 and 743 of the UCC).

436. In the UCC, there are some rules common to these three ways of movable accession. In all the cases in which materials had been used without the knowledge of his owner, and he has the right to the property of the thing resulting from the use of these materials, he can renounce it and ask that instead of his materials, some of the same nature, quality and aptitude be returned to him, or he can ask for their value in money (Article 744 of the UCC). But if the owner of the materials knew about the use of his materials by someone else, it will be presumed that he consented this use, and will only have the right to its value (Article 745 of the UCC).

437. He who knew that the materials belonged to the other person when using them, and used them without the knowledge of the owner, will always lose his own materials or work, and will have to pay for the damages caused to the owner, notwithstanding the criminal action that might be brought by the owner (Article 746 of the UCC). Finally, in all the cases in which the thing becomes joint property of the owners of the materials of it, the thing can be sold for their benefit (Article 747 of the UCC).

Chapter 5. Appropriation

438. The occupancy, also known as appropriation, is a way to acquire property and is regulated by Articles 706–730 of the UCC. Through occupancy, it is only possible to obtain the domain of movable property that does not have an owner due to the fact that they never belonged to a person, or because they had an owner, but he abandoned them. It is a way to acquire the possession and the property (through occupancy it is not possible to acquire other real or personal rights). It is characterized by the entry in possession with the thing subject to occupancy, that can only take place by the material grabbing of the thing, without being required, though it usually exists, the intent of owning it (animus occupandi). The occupancy is a way of obtaining the possession and eventually the property of a thing. Usually, the acquisition of both occurs simultaneously (as happens with the wild animals and the abandoned things), but the UCC mentions some cases in which the possession can be acquired without acquiring the property of the thing: e.g., if the person thinks that a thing is abandoned and it is actually lost.[66]

439. Article 706 of the UCC states that occupancy is a way of acquiring the domain of things that do not belong to anyone, and which acquisition is not forbidden by local or by international laws. Immovables cannot be acquired by occupancy. Regarding this issue, it is important to point out that in virtue of Articles 481 and 482 of the UCC, all the land that does not have an owner belongs to the State, and the vacant things, and those of a person who dies without leaving heirs, also belong to the State.

440. The Code mentions as types of occupancies the hunting and the fishing, as well as the discovery. Notwithstanding this, the rights regarding things thrown into the sea, or that the sea throws to the shore, whatever its nature, are regulated by other special, specific laws. It is also regulated by special laws, the occupancy during war (Articles 706 and 707 of the UCC).

441. Articles 708–716 regulate the occupancy through hunting and fishing, while Articles 717–730 regulate the cases of discovery.

442. Things are not subject to occupancy, if, notwithstanding not belonging to anybody, it can be understood that they do belong to someone, either because they are not the kind of things that one abandons, nor they are *res nullius*. If someone finds these kinds of things, he must hand it over to the nearest judge of the place where the thing was found. After receiving it, the judge will make publications informing about the finding, and, if a year passes by and no one claims to own it, the judge will sell it, and from the amount received for the thing, the judge will deduct the expenses incurred by the Court and will divide the remaining in equal parts between the person who found the thing and the Municipality of the Department (Article 726 of the UCC).

---

66. Howard, Walter, *supra*, p. 49.

443. But if, after the publications, the owner of the thing appears, the thing founded will be returned to him, but he will have to pay the expenses made by the Court for the publications, maintenance of the thing, etc. Also, the owner will have to pay the finder what the judge fixes as a reward. If the owner had offered a reward for the finding of the thing, the finder will have to choose between the amount fixed by the judge and the one offered by the owner (Article 727 of the UCC). But if the person who founds the thing did not give it to the nearest judge, he will lose this award, might be condemned to pay for the damages caused, and also might be criminally accused of misappropriation.

444. Finally, if the thing is sold in auction before the owner appears, the owner will lose it irrevocably (Article 728 of the UCC). Nevertheless, if the thing was perishable or its custody or conservation was too difficult, the auction can be anticipated, and the price obtained will be deposited in the Court's account, and will be delivered to the owner, if he shows up before a year passes since the publications (Article 729 of the UCC).

Chapter 6. Expropriation

445. The expropriation is an institute of public law by which the administration, for the compliance of public aims, acquires in a coercive way movable or immovable, corporeal or incorporeal things, following a certain procedure and paying a just and previous compensation. The entity which decides the expropriation must be a state entity.[67]

446. Article 32 of the Uruguayan Constitution states that "Property is an inviolable right, subject to what the laws establish for reasons of general interest. No one can be deprived from his right of property but in the cases of public necessity or public utility established by a law, and always receiving from the National Treasure a just and previous compensation. When the expropriation, due to public necessity or public utility is declared, the owners will be compensated for the damages they suffered due to the duration of the expropriatory proceeding, even those damages that are generated due to the currency variations, notwithstanding, if the expropriation is performed or not."

447. The expropriation is regulated by Law 3,958, dated March 28, 1912. The proceeding to expropriate a thing starts with an administrative decision which determines the thing to be expropriated. In the national field, the decision has to be taken by the Executive Power. In the municipal area, the decision is taken by the Department Council (Consejo Departamental), with the Department Committee's (Junta) consent. The only things that can be expropriated are those that the law has qualified for public necessity or public utility. The administration decision, with the identification of the things to be expropriated, must be published in the State Official Gazette and in a newspaper of the Department where the thing is located.

448. This decision can be appealed first before the administration, and then before Court. After the decision has become final, the administration starts the proceeding to establish the just compensation for the thing, through the valuation of the thing. After this, the notary public of the administration that is expropriating the thing drafts the deed, which transfers the property of the thing to the administration. Afterward, the parties sign it and the just compensation is paid. If the expropriated party refuses to sign the deed, the administration can ask the judge to act as a representative of the owner of the thing subject to expropriation, and sign the deed on his behalf.[68]

67. Sayagues Laso, Enrique, "Tratado de Derecho Administrativo," Editorial Fundación de Cultura Universitaria, 1988, pp. 312–313.
68. Sayagues Laso, Enrique, *supra*, pp. 361–364.

Chapter 7. Insolvency

449. In Uruguayan law, matters referred to insolvency are regulated in Law 18.387, issued on October 23, 2008, amended afterward by Acts 18.593 and 18.937 and called Judicial Declaration of Bankruptcy, and Business Reorganization Law. This Act applies to any debtor who is in state of insolvency. It is considered state of insolvency, the impossibility of a debtor to pay his debts (Article 1 of the law). This judicial declaration of bankruptcy will proceed regarding any debtor, physical persons who perform business activity or legal person (which can be civil or commercial) (Article 2 of the law.) This act does not apply to the Uruguayan State, Autonomous Agencies, Decentralized Services, Department Governments and the financial intermediation entities. Insolvency cases of physical persons, which are not included in this law, are regulated by the General Proceeding Code.

450. The main objective of the Act under the modern insolvency system is to reduce the number of insolvent companies in favor of preserving the value of businesses through corporate restructurings.[69]

451. The Court declares bankruptcy if the debtor is insolvent (Article 1 of the law). The state of insolvency takes place when a debtor cannot pay all his debts (even if the creditor is only one person or legal entity). The declaration of bankruptcy will be voluntary, when it is requested by the debtor, and necessary, if it is requested by the creditors.

452. The insolvency proceeding has three stages. At any stage, the debtor can enter into a private, out of court agreement, with creditors, in order to avoid the liquidation of the company's assets. In case an agreement is signed, this agreement will only bind the parties who have signed it. The proceeding can end with one of the following outcomes: (i) agreement with creditors: the debtor and creditors negotiate and enter into an agreement to restructure the business with a plan that may feature any of the following: (a) partial discharge of creditor claims; (b) extension of the debtor's maturity terms; (c) assignment of assets to creditors; (d) formation of a company made up of creditors without any preferred claims; (e) debt capitalization; (f) formation of a trust; (g) company reorganization; or (h) partial or complete asset management in benefit of the creditors; (ii) selling the business as a going concern; or (iii) selling the business into different pieces. In this case, the Act encourages sales of the business in "productive units."

453. After the Bankruptcy Court declares a debtor insolvent, it will appoint a receiver, who will manage the debtor's assets and creditor's claims. He can act

69. Ferreira, Hector, "The Nuts and Bolts of Uruguayan Insolvency and Bankruptcy Laws," https://www.clearygottlieb.com/~/media/organize-archive/cgsh/files/emerging-markets-restructuring-journal/emrj-issue-2-fall-2016/05-the-nuts-and-bolts-of-uruguayan-insolvency-and-bankruptcy-laws.pdf.

alone, or with the participation of the debtor. The company's directors and management may or may not be removed once a receiver is appointed. A registry of receivers was created under the supervision of the Bankruptcy Court, and receivers included in this registry will remain in their positions for a period of four years.

454. According to Article 171 of the law, the bankrupt entity should be sold as a whole. In case this is not possible, the receiver must try to sell the productive units of the business, unless it is more convenient for the creditors to sell the different assets separately.

455. The sale of the assets will be performed according to the law applicable to execution proceedings (Articles 377 and following of the CGP). This is an original mode of acquisition since assets are acquired free from encumbrances (Article 389 of the CGP).

456. The sale of the assets in the bankruptcy proceeding will take place through an auction (Article 385 of the CGP).

Chapter 8. Acquisition Ministerio Legis

457. In Uruguay, there are plenty of cases in which the property of a thing or of a right is acquired "by operation of the law" (or by "ministerio legis"). An example of this is the case referred to in Article 481 of the UCC, which states that all the land that does not have an owner belongs to the State. Another example is Article 482 of the UCC, which establishes that the things of a person who dies without leaving heirs also belong to the State.

458. One more example of acquisition ministerio legis is the one established in Articles 1941 and 1955 of the UCC, which determines that if the spouses do not establish a different regime, then after marrying, they will be owners of half of the things obtained while being married.

Part IV. Trust and Fiduciary Mechanisms

Chapter 1. Introduction

459. The economic context presents a scenario in which universal access to credit is increasingly sought, but at the same time, the credit guarantees in case of nonpayment are usually insufficient. Businesses seek to have access to credit, by offering as guarantee their **fixed** assets (which are usually the only assets a businessman can offer), but these assets as guarantees have proven to be inefficient, due to various causes: difficulties in the judicial execution, existence of other preferential guarantees, the bankruptcy of the debtor, etc., which in all cases affect the payment of the debt subject to guarantee.[70]

460. As many scholars have pointed out, this is the base of the so-called crisis of the real guarantees. Indeed, the traditional guarantees have been left aside in the new commercial transactions, seeking new solutions that adapt to this necessity of liquidity and security in compliance. In other words, these new solutions seek to maintain and widen the access to credit, but diversify the usual numerous clausus system of the guarantees.

461. Together with this, the traditional systems of patrimonial administration (one person equals one patrimony) also become insufficient in today's business world, in which several aims are sought through the combination of different legal instruments.

462. In this state of things, trust arises as the legal transaction suitable to be applied to the modern phenomena of guarantee and of administration, giving them flexibility and a wide margin for the execution of deals. The contract of trust seeks, among others, the administration of things, to help recover a company in crisis, etc.

463. The contract of trust has its origins in the Roman law, in which "fiducia" meant trust. Meanwhile, the word "fideicomiso" (trust) comes from the Latin word "fideicommissum," which is composed of "fides" and "commisus," which means faith and the person in which one trusts, respectively. The trust in Roman times was a contract by which one party, the fiduciante or fideicomitente (trustor), delivered a

70. Pallas, Nicolás, "Manual de Contratos," Volume II, coordinated by Beatriz Venturini, Editorial University of Montevideo, pp. 463–466.

thing to the other party, the fiduciario (trustee), who, after receiving it, assumed the obligation to use it with a specific aim and to give it back once the aim was accomplished.

464. There were two kinds of trust contracts in these times: (i) the fiducia cum amico: which was a transaction for administration (collaboration) based purely on trust, where a thing was transferred in property to another person in order for him to perform a specific request, usually of custody or use, and then transfer its property to the former owner. This contract was based on the trust the parties had for each other, and was not protected with any legal action in case of breach; (ii) on the other hand, the fiducia cum creditore was a guarantee transaction, by which the debtor transferred the property of things he owned to his creditor, so that if he did not comply with his obligation, the creditor would become the owner of these things.

465. Roman law also had the figure of the testamentary trust, where the testator left the property of all or part of his things to a person so that he could use them according to the testator's instructions.[71]

466. This kind of trust differs from the trust of the Germanic law (which afterward was adopted by English law) in that the Germanic trust transfers the property of the things but under a resolutory condition, after which the property returns to the former owner. Germanic law even establishes the possibility to vindicate the things subject to trust from third parties. This way, the property right for the first time is divided, turning the trustee into material owner, while the trustor continues being the formal owner. It is also the first time the concept of "affected patrimony" is used.

467. According to the Common Law (Restatement of the Law of Trusts), trust is the relationship regarding specific things, by which the person who possesses them (trustee) is bound in law and equity to manage them in benefit of a third party. This transaction occurs as a result of an express volitive act of the person who creates the trust (trustor).

71. Pallas, Nicolás, "Manual de Contratos," *supra*, pp. 467–468.

Chapter 2. Law 17,703 and Features of the Trust

468. Before Law 17,703, trust contracts were already executed in Uruguay, mainly in the Successory Law, where the trust was used, in order for the testator to leave some instructions which sought, in most cases, to elude forced heirs and forced heirship. Because of this, Articles 865 and 866 of the UCC forbid testamentary trusts. This prohibition was abrogated by Law 17,703, which regulated the testamentary trust. Also, before being regulated, trust was common in family law, where an affected patrimony was created to benefit minors or incompetents, and a professional (trustee) was appointed to administer this patrimony.[72]

469. Law 17,703 regulated for the first time in Uruguay the trust, and in its Article 1 defined it as "the legal transaction by which a property held in trust is constituted over a group of property rights or other real or personal rights, which are transferred by the trustor to the trustee so that he can administer them or use them according to the instructions contained in the trust, in benefit of a person (beneficiary), which is appointed in the trust, and give it back to the trustor, or transfer it to the beneficiary, after the period of time agreed comes to an end or the condition agreed upon occurs."

470. After the trust is executed, a patrimony is created, which is different from the patrimony of the trustor and of the trustee. The unitary concept of patrimony established by Article 2372 of the UCC is altered,[73] due to the fact that the assets of the patrimony affected will not be the guarantee of the creditors of any of the three individuals involved. The creditors of the trustee cannot attack those assets subject to trust, nor can the creditors of the trustor (who can, nevertheless, claim that the trustor committed fraud when constituting the trust). Finally, the creditors of the beneficiary can only seize the fruits of the patrimony affected by the trust. The only creditors that can attack these assets are the creditors of the patrimony subject to trust (when the administration of the assets generates obligations).

471. Another feature of the trust is that it is not perpetual. The fiduciary property is created to be extinguished eventually. It is not perpetual, as common property. The trustee does not have the property indefinitely. He must detach from this property after the purpose for which it was created is obtained, or when the period of time fixed is due, or when the condition under which it was created happens, or when whatever of the causes for the end of the trust occurs. Anyhow, it can never last longer than thirty years, which is the maximum period established by Article 33 b) of Law 17.703.

72. Pallas, Nicolás, "Manual de Contratos," *supra*, pp. 467–468.
73. Article 2372 of the UCC states that "All the assets of the debtor, except for those that cannot be subject to seizure, are the guarantee of his creditors, (…)."

Chapter 3. Requirements for the Validity of the Trust

472. The requirements for the validity of the trust are the following: consent, capacity, lawful object and cause, and the inclusion of some necessary clauses, under penalty of absolute nullity. Regarding consent, Article 2 of the law states that the will of the parties must be documented in writing, which is considered by scholars as a solemnity requirement. The law also states that the trust must be documented in a public deed when the law determines so. There is no provision that states which trust contracts must be made in a public deed,[74] but it can be understood that it refers to the cases in which an immovable thing, an easement, rent charges or inheritance successions must be sold or purchased (which must be documented in a public deed, according to Article 1664 of the UCC).

473. Regarding the capacity to contract, in the case of trust, if the contract is *inter vivos* (between living parties), then the parties must have legal age to contract (18 years), but if the trust is established by testament, then the capacity of the trustor is the one established by the UCC to make a will, which is 12 years for woman and 14 years for men.

474. The third requirement for the validity of the will refers to the licit object and licit cause. The trust can be established over corporeal or incorporeal things, present or future, or even over a group of things and rights when it refers to a testamentary trust. For the contract to be valid, rights and things subject to the trust as well as the interest pursued must be licit, determined or subject to determination.

475. The fourth and last element for the validity of the contract consists in the clauses required by Article 4 of Law 17,703, under penalty of nullity. These clauses are the following: (i) the individualization of the things or rights subject to trust. If this is not possible at the time of the trust, a description must be made of the requirements and features that these things or rights must have; (ii) the determination of the proceeding in which the things or rights can be incorporated into the trust (floating trust); (iii) the term or condition to which the trust property is subject (in case it is not determined, the maximum term of thirty years will apply); (iv) the destiny of the assets when the trust is over (in case this is not established, the law states that the assets will return to the trustor); and finally, (v) the rights and obligations of the trustee and the way to substitute him in case the trustee ceases from his functions.

74. Pallas, Nicolás, "Manual de Contratos," *supra*, pp. 472–473.

Chapter 4. Types of Trust

476. The trust can be of two kinds for its creation, *inter vivos* (between living parties) or by will. Through an act between living parties, the trust is a title able to transfer the property of the things and rights subject to trust. In this case, the transfer of property requires the obligational transaction (trust contract) and the dispositive legal act (tradition, inscription of the trust). Meanwhile, the testamentary trust can be established by will (which can be an open or a closed will), complying with the statutory provisions for the making of the will. The transfer of the things and rights which belonged to the testator and where subject to trust will occur through the succession proceeding.

Also, according to their function, there are also three kinds of trusts: the administration trust, the guarantee trust and the financial trust.[75]

§1. Administration of Property: Fiducia Cum Amico

477. The administration trust is similar to the fiducia cum amico. In it, assets are transferred to the trustee, in custody, so that the trustee can manage or use them in a certain way. Here, the trustee uses the real right, but with the limits established in the contract, which bounds him to administer the trust property as if it still belonged to the trustor.

§2. Security: Fiducia Cum Creditore (*See Also* Part I, II and V)

478. The guarantee trust, as it used to happen in the fiducia cum creditore, consists in a trust, in which the trustor transfers an asset to the trustee, in guarantee of an obligation, and the trustee agrees to return it after the trustor complies with the obligation assumed. Also, the trust must establish the steps to take in case of noncompliance, a case in which the trustee must proceed to the sale of the assets subject to trust, in order to cancel the whole or part of the debt with the product of the sale.

479. Finally, in the financial trust, there is a transfer of the property or assets to an affected patrimony, but the difference is that this patrimony is administered by a financial intermediation institution, which, at the same time, issues titles representative of the different rights: participation titles (each of them represents a part of the patrimony), debt titles (guarantee in the assets), and a combined title.

75. Pallas, Nicolás, "Manual de Contratos," *supra*, pp. 473–474.

Chapter 5. Extinction of the Trust

480. Article 33 of Law 17,703 establishes that the causes of extinction of the trusts are the following: (i) the total compliance with the purpose of the trust, or the absolute impossibility to achieve it; (ii) the ending of the term of the trust, or the occurrence of the resolutory condition stipulated in the trust. As was already mentioned, if a term was not stipulated in the trust, then the maximum term possible is of thirty years. Any resolutory condition on which the return of the assets depends on, which did not occur after thirty years from the date of the trust, will be understood to have happened after these thirty years have passed; (iii) the agreement between the trustor and the beneficiary, without prejudice of the rights of the trustee; (iv) the cease in the payment of its obligations, unless the case of the financial trust; (v) the revocation of the trustor, if he expressly reserved this right in the trust; (vi) in case of resolution of the assembly of holders of debt titles, adopted in the terms and conditions established in Article 32 of Law 17,703; (vii) in the case of death or disability legally declared of the trustee, unless in the contract of trust the trustor appointed a substitute trustee; (viii) due to any other cause established in the trust contract.

481. After the extinction of the contract occurs, the trustee must deliver the trust property to the trustor or to his successors, unless the other thing is established in the contract of trust. In case the trustee ceases, and if a substitute was appointed, the delivery of the trust property occurs automatically, unless the extinction of the trust occurs due to noncompliance with the payments agreed. In no event will the trustee be able to appropriate, in a definite way, the assets of the trust property.

Chapter 6. Sale with Clause of Selling Back to the Vendor

482. Articles 1748–1754 regulate the sale with the clause of selling back to the vendor. This clause causes an effect similar to the one of the trust, in which the things and rights subject to trust, after a term of time or the occurrence of a condition, must go back to the trustor.

483. In this case, the seller keeps the right to rebuy the object sold under certain conditions. In case the seller decides to rebuy the property, he will have to pay the buyer the amount established by the parties, or the price of the purchase (Article 1748 of the UCC).

484. The seller will have the right to receive the property with its accessories and to be compensated for the damages suffered by the property due to the negligence of the buyer. On the other hand, the seller must pay the buyer for the necessary expenses, but not for the ones invested in useful improvements, when they were done without his consent. The fruits of the thing sold will be compensated with the interests of the price of the sale.

485. The seller will have a maximum term of three years, since the day of the signing of the purchase contract, to apply the selling back clause. But the buyer shall receive a previous notice that cannot be of less than ninety days, for real estate, and fifteen days for movable objects, and if the thing was fructiferous, and did not give fruits but from time to time, and due to work and investments made in order to prepare it for it, then it cannot be required to be returned until the perception of the fruits has happened (Article 1754 of the UCC). Finally, this clause is not opposable to third parties acting with good faith (Article 1752).

Part V. Security

Chapter 1. Introduction

486. In this chapter, we will analyze all the mechanisms that, with erga omnes efficacy, are used to guarantee a credit. The guarantee contracts constitute a way to protect a credit. This obligation consists in a legal relationship which binds two individuals (creditor and debtor) and in which the creditor is the holder of a right (credit) and the debtor complies with a specific obligation (debt), and in case he does not comply, the creditor is protected by the legal system, through the procedure of forced execution.

487. The breach of contract is closely related to the concept of liability, which in ancient times had as object the person of the debtor, but now refers to his patrimony. Indeed, according to Article 2372 of the UCC, "all the assets of the debtor, except for the ones that cannot be seized (Article 2363), are the common guarantee of his creditors (…)."[76]

488. Hence, when a debtor does not pay a debt due, the creditor can request before a Court the seizure of his assets. These assets can be movable or immovable. The movable assets can refer to banking accounts. The debtor's assets will be sold in auction, in order for the creditors to collect the money owed to them.

489. When a debtor has more than one creditor and all of them sue him for the payment of their credits, and the assets of the debtor are not enough to pay all these debts, then the creditors will receive a part of the debtor's assets, in proportion to their debts (and under the same rules as the other creditors). This is commonly called the rule of par condicio creditorum (equal treatment of creditors).

490. One exception to this rule is the one established in the second paragraph of Article 242 of Law 18,387 (Law of Insolvency and Business Reorganization), which states that: "There will be no distinction in the treatment of the national and foreign creditors, unless in the labor credits with general privilege, which will have preference in its collection over the assets located in national territory. When it is proven

76. Gamarra, Jorge, "Tratado de Derecho Civil Uruguayo," Second Volume, *supra*, pp. 7–8.

that in the State of the domicile of the debtor, the Uruguayan creditors are not admitted in the same conditions as the national ones, the reciprocity principle will apply. The principle of reciprocity will not apply in the case of credits guaranteed with pledges or mortgages."

491. Another exception to this general rule of par condicion creditorum is the one referred to as real rights of guarantee. In effect, some creditors can get in a better position than the others in the collection of their debts, through the creation of real rights of guarantee. If a real right of guarantee is constituted by the debtor, then when the debt is due, if the debtor does not pay it, the creditor can ask for the sale in an auction, of the property subject to this guarantee, and collect his debt from the product of this sale. This will happen, regardless of the other debts the debtor might have, and regardless of how limited the debtor's patrimony might be with regard to the debts he has. This will happen even if the property subject to guarantee is sold to a third party (because the guarantee will continue attached to the property subject to the real right of guarantee), and even in case of bankruptcy of the debtor.

492. Besides the real rights of guarantee, there are other mechanisms that also position the creditor in a better place in order to collect his debt from the debtor. An example of this is the retention right, which allows a creditor to withhold a thing under his control, until the debtor pays his debt. This happens, for example, in the case of the vindication of a thing, in which in order to recover the thing, the owner must pay the expenses incurred by the current possessor of the thing in order to make useful improvements to it, which increased its value. The expenses owed are the ones incurred before answering the complaint. Until the owner pays these expenses, the actual possessor can retain the thing vindicated (Article 699 of the UCC).

493. Another case in which a creditor is better positioned than the rest of the creditors with respect to the debtor is the case in which the debtors' assets are not enough to pay all his debts, and one creditor has a credit with the debtor, but also owes him money, at the same time. In this case, and as long as both debts comply with the requirements of law (the object of the two debts must be of the same kind, both must be liquid, they must be claimable and must be personal), they can be compensated (Article 65 of Act 18,387). But in order for the credits to be compensated, they must meet the requirements aforementioned before the debtor is declared insolvent.

494. Finally, another way for a creditor to be in a better position regarding other creditors is the personal guarantees, such as the debt in which the debtor is guaranteed by a guarantor. In this case, the creditor will have two patrimonies to guarantee the payment of his debt, and will not depend exclusively on the patrimony of the debtor, to satisfy his interests.

Chapter 2. Securities in Immovable Property (*See Also* Parts I and IV)

§1. PRIVILEGES, LIENS, AND CHARGES

I. Introduction

495. In Uruguayan law, we can find guarantees that fall upon immovable property, and guarantee the payment of a debt, or place the creditor in a better position than other creditors in the satisfaction of his credit.

II. Immovable Privileges

496. Law 18,387 (called Law of Bankruptcy and Business Reorganization) establishes different categories of credits, after a debtor becomes insolvent. The credits, according to Article 108 of this law, will be classified into privileged credits, common credits (quirografarios) and subordinate credits. The privileged credits are subclassified as well, into credits with special privileges and credits with general privileges.

497. The credits with special privileges are those guaranteed with pledge or mortgage (Article 109 of Law 18,387). But the law states that these credits must be registered in the Public Registry before the date of the declaration of insolvency, except for the common pledge contracts, which must have been executed in a public document, or in a private document with a date certain.

498. When a credit has a pledge or mortgage, it excludes all the other credits to the extent of its amount (Article 92 of Law 18,387).

499. After declaring the bankruptcy of the debtor, no creditor can start new executions against the debtor for credits incurred before the declaration, and those executions which are being processed, as well as the seizures that have been ordered, will be suspended (third paragraph of Article 225). Therefore, those immovable properties subject to seizure will become part of the assets of the debtor in the bankruptcy proceeding, and the seizures ordered by Courts will not give a privilege to the creditor over the property seized.

III. Securities in the Sale on Credit of Immovable Goods

500. Uruguayan law provides two ways to guarantee the transfer of the property to the prospective buyer and a way to guarantee the payment of the deferred price to the prospective seller, in sales on credit of immovable properties (called promesa de enajenación de inmuebles a plazos). This contract is regulated by Law 8733, enacted in 1931.

501. It is important to point out that before this law, the person who agreed to buy a real estate in instalments (called prospective buyer) did not have legal protection regarding third parties. He was the holder of a personal right, which constituted the right to receive an obligation to do (because the prospective seller agreed to transfer the property of the real estate subject to contract after the payment of the whole price). Being a personal right, it could not be opposed to third parties.

502. But Law 8733 granted the prospective buyer a real right in order to guarantee this personal right. This generated a strengthening of the credit of the prospective buyer. This real right, after being registered in the Property National Registry, was opposable to third parties.

503. The second way to guarantee the transfer of the real estate is the specific forced execution, which allows the judge to substitute the party who refuses to comply with his obligation, in order to transfer the property of the real estate.

504. It is also important to point out that regarding the payment of the price of the real estate, Law 8733 also provides a guarantee. This is so because, before this law, Article 1732 of the UCC was the rule to apply to this type of contract, and stated that "The clause that establishes that the property will not be transferred until the payment of the price is made, will not produce other effect than the one stated above," and in the preceding article, it stated that "If the buyer defaults in the payment of the price in the time and place agreed upon, the seller will have the right to require the price or rescind the purchase agreement, and can ask for a compensation for the damages suffered." Therefore, until the enactment of this law, the reservation of dominion over property given or retention of title-clause was forbidden.

IV. The Real Burden in the Joint Ownership of Blocks of Flats

505. The joint ownership of flats, as was mentioned above, is regulated by the so-called Law of Horizontal Property (Law 10,751). The owners of these properties have two kinds of rights: the right of property over their premises and the joint ownership of the common elements of the building. The owner of a property under this regime has the duty to contribute to the payment of the "common expenses" for the administration, maintenance, repair and insurance of the building. This contribution will be calculated taking into account the value of each flat unless parties agree otherwise (Article 5 of Law 10,751).

506. The common expenses owed by a co-owner, calculated by the manager of the building and approved by the co-owners assembly, will constitute an enforcement title (and therefore, the proceeding for the collection of it will be much faster and simpler, in application of Article 14 of Law 14,560).

507. Finally, Article 6 of Law 14,261 states that each of the units of the building will be automatically mortgaged in favor of the other co-owners, in guarantee of the common expenses of the building. This mortgage will not guarantee more than 30% of the fiscal value of each flat, will be documented in the co-ownership regulations, and will be registered in the Mortgage Registry of the place where the building is. This mortgage is known in Uruguayan law as the reciprocal mortgage.

§2. MORTGAGE

I. Concept and General Features

508. The mortgage is a real right guarantee which falls upon immovable things. For this real right to be constituted, the mortgage contract must be executed in a public deed, and it must be registered in the Property Registry, in the section of immovables (Article 2323 of the UCC).

509. The real right of mortgage allows its holder to ask before Court the auction of the immovable mortgaged, in order to cover with the product of the auction the guaranteed obligation. Mortgage is regulated by Articles 2322–2348 of the UCC and by Articles 766–787 of the Commercial Code. Besides this, there are other rules regarding mortgage worth mentioning, such as Law 18,387 (the law of Bankruptcy and Business Reorganization), which refers to mortgage in cases such as Article 113, in which it establishes that mortgages will be canceled when it is proven that the creditor is related to the debtor, and Article 109 which states that the credits guaranteed by mortgage will be considered special privileged credits, among others.

510. The mortgage is a real right. The owner of the property mortgaged continues being the owner of it, and continues using and enjoying the thing. This happens due to the fact that the mortgage does not entail the transfer of the possession of the property mortgaged. The owner can even sell the property mortgaged and can constitute real rights in it. But if he sells it, the property will be transferred with the mortgage, and the buyer will have to assume the risk of losing his property, in case the mortgager does not comply with his obligation.

511. The principal feature of the mortgage is the possibility of the mortgager to ask judicially for the sale of the property mortgaged, in case the mortgager does not pay his debt. In case the property is sold in an auction, the product of this sale will first serve to cover the unpaid debt, and the remainder will go to the owner. The mortgage is accessory to the obligation it guarantees. Therefore, in case the credit (main obligation) is paid, this entails the extinction of the mortgage. On the other hand, the mortgagee can never transfer the limited right of mortgage, without transferring the credit it guarantees.

II. Subjects and Object

512. In a mortgage relationship, there must be at least two persons: the mortgagee (the holder of the credit guaranteed by the mortgage) and the owner of the mortgaged property, who usually is the mortgager, but could also be a third party (due to the fact that he accepted to mortgage his property to guarantee someone else's debt, or because he bought the property already mortgaged). The owner, in order to constitute mortgage over his property, must have the legal capacity to transfer the property. The beneficial owner of a usufruct can also mortgage the property, but the mortgage will refer only to usufruct, and will not comprise the bare ownership. Finally, it is not necessary that at the time of the creation of the mortgage the owner has the possession of the property mortgaged.

513. Regarding the object of the mortgage, the rule is that only immovable property can be subject to mortgage (Articles 2322 and 2331 of the UCC). Exceptionally, some movable things can be mortgaged: the ships (Article 2331 of the UCC) and the airplanes (Article 45 of the Aeronautic Code, Law-Decree 14,305 dated November 29, 1974). Therefore, the feature that distinguishes this real right form others does not refer to the nature of the thing, but to the possibility to identify it, which allows the possibility to register it. Nevertheless, this criterion did not apply in the case of other identifiable things, such as automobiles, in which the legislator preferred the guarantee of the pledge without displacement. The mortgage can also fall upon floating dams (Article 2331 of the UCC). Also, it is important to point out that future things cannot be subject to mortgage (Article 2332 of the UCC).

514. Although the right of property is the principal right subject to mortgage, other real rights, such as easements and usufructs, can also be mortgaged. But in this case, the mortgager cannot mortgage a right wider than the one he has (Article 2329 of the UCC).

515. Regarding the mortgage reach, Article 2335 of the UCC states that the mortgage will extend to all the accessories and improvements made over the thing. It will also extend over the compensation owed by an insurance company in case the thing suffered damages. It also affects the fruits of the thing, which are pending to be collected at the time the creditor exercises his mortgage rights (Article 2335 of the UCC).

III. Extent of the Mortgage Related to the Guaranteed Obligation

516. The UCC forbids that a mortgage is established for more than twice the amount of the obligation, which must be clearly stated in the public deed. Scholars in Uruguay have discussed what must be understood as "the amount of the obligation." Some of them understand that the amount of the obligation is the amount without the interests agreed by the parties (remuneratory interest), while others state that the amount of the obligation is the equivalent to the amount of the credit plus the interests agreed. The latter is the position that maintains, among others, Professor Jorge Gamarra.[77]

IV. Content of the Right

517. The mortgage is a real right that has two phases. The first phase is the one in which the obligation guaranteed is not yet due. The second phase occurs when the obligation is due, and the mortgager cannot pay his credit.

518. In the first phase, and due to the fact that the mortgage does not entail the transfer of the property, the law allows the mortgagee to ask for an improvement of the guarantee, if the property mortgaged is lost or damaged in a way it is not sufficient anymore to cover the amount of the obligation. In case the debtor does not improve the guarantee, or gives the creditor an equivalent guarantee, the mortgagee can ask for the payment of the whole debt, even if it is not due yet.

519. Regarding the second phase, the mortgagee must request before Uruguayan Courts the start of the execution procedure (Articles 371–401 of the General Proceeding Code). For this proceeding to be started, the debtor must have renounced the right to be sued in an executive procedure (which usually happens). If the debtor did not make this renunciation, then the mortgagee must sue him according to the rules of the executive procedure (the one applicable, among others, to securities, and regulated by Articles 353–362 of the General Procedure Code).

520. In the execution procedure, after the mortgagee files the claim, the debtor will have ten days to file his defense writ. He can only interrupt this proceeding, by arguing and proving the following that: (i) he already paid his debt and (ii) the mortgage contract is not valid. In case these defenses are not filed, or the judge dismisses them based on lack of evidence, the judge will order the seizure of the property. The seizure will be registered in the Immovables Registry.

521. After the seizure of the property is made, the owner must deliver the titles of the property in a period of five days. If the title is in the power of a third party, the judge will request this person to deliver the titles in the period mentioned above.

522. After this, the mortgagee will file in Court the registry certificates, and a notary certificate containing the study of the property titles made by the notary of the mortgagee. The court clerk afterward will have twenty days to control this study, and will also inform the Court about other creditors who have rights over the property mortgaged (other mortgages, seizures, etc.).

523. After the Court has approved the titles, and after the mortgagee requests it, the Court will order the auction of the mortgaged property. Once the auction is over,

77. Gamarra, Jorge, "Tratado de Derecho Civil Uruguayo," Second Volume, *supra*, pp. 269–271.

the price paid by the buyer of the mortgaged property will be applied first to the payment of the credit of the holder of the mortgage or seizure which was first registered in the immovable registry, and afterward, to the following mortgages, seizures, etc., in case they exist. Afterward, the remaining will be delivered to the mortgager, or to the current owner of the property, in case it belonged to someone else.

V. Assignment of the Mortgage Credit and Sale of the Mortgaged Estate

524. As was mentioned before, the mortgager as well as the mortgagee can transfer their respective rights. The mortgager can transfer the property, usufruct, or real right he has mortgaged to a third party, and the mortgagee can transfer the obligation guaranteed to someone else (Article 2339 of the UCC).

525. In the first case, as was already mentioned, the new owner of the property will buy the thing with the encumbrance, and, therefore, will accept the risk of losing it in case the debtor does not pay his debt. But the new owner will not assume the responsibility of paying the debt guaranteed with the mortgage, and will only respond up to the value of the property mortgaged. In Uruguay, it is common that, when a property is sold with a mortgage, the parties agree that the buyer retains part of the price for the payment of the debt guaranteed with the mortgage, or discounts from the total price the amount of the debt guaranteed, so that this way, he guarantees the payment of the said debt, and avoids the possibility of losing the property bought.

526. In the second case, the mortgagee, after transferring his credit, guaranteed by the mortgage, will have to notify the mortgager of this transfer. If after being notified, the debtor accepts the transfer, he will be renouncing to oppose to the new holder of the credit, the personal defenses he could oppose to the former holder. But if he refuses to accept this transfer, he will be able to oppose to the new holder of the credit, the same defenses he could have opposed to the original holder (such as the compensation of debts). The transfer of the credit must be made in a public deed and registered in the National Registry of Property (Immovables section). If the mortgager is not notified of the transfer of the credit, and this transfer is not registered, and he pays directly to the mortgagee, he will have complied with his obligation, and the new holder of the credit will only have a legal action against the mortgagee.

Chapter 3. Securities in Movable Property (*See Also* Parts II and IV)

527. In this chapter, we will examine institutions used to guarantee the payment of a debt, or to give a creditor a preference for the payment of his debt in relation to other creditors, through the encumbrance of movable things.

§1. Privileges, Liens, and Charges

I. Movable Privileges

528. Movable things can be encumbered by pledges and by pledges without displacement. The creditor holder of the pledge will have a preference for the collection of his debt, for up to the value of the movable thing at stake. Notwithstanding this, there are other cases in which creditors have a preference for the collection of their debt, regarding the other creditors, in relation to a specific thing. For example, when a movable thing is sold by someone different from the owner to a third party, the owner can request for the thing to be returned to him, but previously he will have to pay the buyer the useful expenses and the improvements made by the buyer to the thing. Until he pays these amounts, the buyer will have the right to withhold the thing. Another case where the right of retention applies is the case of the contract of bailment, in which the bailor of a thing has to spend from his own money to preserve the thing subject to custody. Until the bailee does not pay the amount spent on the preservation of the thing, the custodian has a right to keep it (Article 2271 of the UCC).

529. When two or more pledges without displacements (registered in the National Registry of Property) affect the same movable goods in a debtor's patrimony, the pledge which was registered before will have priority.

II. Reservation of Domain Clause

530. In Uruguay, it is forbidden to state in a contract, when the price of a movable good is deferred in time, that the thing will not be transferred to the buyer until the price is paid in full (Article 1732 of the UCC).

§2. Pledge

I. Introduction

531. The pledge is a real right because to exist, it requires the delivery of the thing. The pledged thing is delivered to the creditor (Article 2292 of the UCC), but if the parties decide so, it can be delivered to a third party (Article 2300 of the UCC) with whom the parties will celebrate a contract of bailment.

532. The pledge can be constituted, as well as the mortgage, by the debtor or by a third party (Articles 2296 and 2327 of the UCC), and it will only refer to movable things.

533. Notwithstanding this, by Law 17,228 dated January 7, 2000, the pledge without displacement was regulated, allowing the debtor to keep the possession of the thing pledged, which, being identifiable, could be registered in the movables registry. This pledge was regulated, due to the fact that usually the most valuable assets of the debtors were used by them for their business (especially, in cases of debtors dedicated to industrial or agrarian activities), and therefore, when dispossessing them of their property, they could not earn the money needed to pay their debts.

II. Pledge with Possessory Transfer

534. In its origins, the pledge was created as a guarantee real right that fell upon another's movable things in order to guarantee the payment of a debt. It also allowed the holder to withhold the possession of the thing given, and to request its sale in case of noncompliance of the debt guaranteed, in order to satisfy the credit with the money collected from this sale. But the person who constitutes the pledge does not have to be the debtor. It can be a third party who wants to help out the debtor (Article 2296 of the UCC).

535. The creditor only obtains the right to the pledge, when the object subject to pledge is delivered to him or to the bailor appointed by the parties (Article 2300). The pledge does not imply the transfer of property of the pledged things but only the transfer of its possession to the creditor. This guarantees that the creditor will not pledge this movable thing again, or sell it to third parties.

536. The creditor must take care of the thing pledged as a good family father (Article 2304), and he cannot sell or appropriate the thing pledged. He also does not have the right to use the thing, unless the debtor allows him. In this aspect, this contract is similar to the contract of bailment, and the creditor has the same obligations as the bailor (Article 2304 of the UCC). He can only ask for its auction, after the noncompliance of the credit guaranteed by the debtor.

537. The creditor can exercise actions to defend the possession of the thing pledged against third parties, and even against the debtor, until the debt guaranteed is paid (Article 2302 of the UCC).

538. The creditor can withhold the thing pledged, even after the debt guaranteed has been paid, if the creditor had other credits with the debtor, which are: (i) liquid and certain, (ii) incurred after the obligation for which the pledge was constituted; and (iii) became claimable before the payment of the debt guaranteed (Article 2315 of the UCC).

539. Regarding the right to sell the pledged thing, in case of noncompliance of the guaranteed debt, the creditor can request the judicial sale of the pledged thing, which will be carried out through a judicial auction, or can also request the adjudication of the thing at the minimum price admissible, to a third party (Article 2307 of the UCC). The creditor and the debtor can also agree that the thing be sold through a broker (when it has a stock market value) or through an extrajudicial auction (Article 2308 of the UCC).

540. In case the debtor becomes insolvent, the pledge creditor will have a preference in relation to the other creditors, in the collection of his debt (Article 109 of Law 18,387).

III. Movable Securities Without Possessory Transfer

541. Law 17,288, dated January 7, 2000, regulates the pledge without displacement and introduces a new real guarantee regarding movable things. As the pledge, this guarantee allows its holder to ask for the judicial auction of the thing, in case the debtor does not pay his debt on time. But in this case, the creditor will not have the possession of the thing subject to pledge. This guarantee can only fall upon movable things and rights that can be identified (Article 3 of Law 17,228).

542. Due to the fact that the creditor will not have the possession of the things subject to pledge, the law established the obligation to register the contract of pledge without displacement in the National Register of Pledges without Displacement. The only exceptions to this rule are: (i) the pledge over motor vehicles which is registered in the National Register of Motor Vehicles; (ii) the pledge over commercial or industrial establishments, which is registered in the National Register of Commerce; (iii) the pledge over industrial property rights, which is registered in the National Office of Industrial Property; and (iv) the pledge over forests, which is registered in the General Register of Forests of the Forestry Office of the Ministry of Agriculture, Livestock and Fishing.

543. The things subject to pledge can be sold, but the transfer of them cannot be done unless the seller pays its debt to his creditor, unless the creditor consents the transfer of the property of the thing subject to pledge. In this case, the change of owner of the thing must be registered in the National Registry of Pledges without Displacement (Article 10 of Law 17,228).

544. The second paragraph of Article 3 of Law 17,228 allows the parties to establish a floating pledge, in virtue of which the parties can agree that some things that enter into the estate of the debtor are comprised in the pledge, substituting or complementing the original appointed things, and must remain in the same place as the ones already appointed.

§3. RETENTION RIGHT, COMPENSATION

I. Retention Right

545. The retention right is the right by which the law allows the creditors to withhold the possession of a movable thing of his debtor, after the moment in which the goods must be returned, until the debtor pays a debt owed to the creditor.

546. This right is granted to the bailor, for the amounts spent in the preservation of the thing subject to bailment (Article 2271 of the UCC), to the mandatory, regarding the amounts spent for the performing of the mandate, and the amount of his salary (Article 2084 of the UCC) and to the person who performed a work in a movable thing of another person, until the one who asked for this work pays the amount owed for it (Article 1854 of the UCC).

II. Compensation

547. Compensation occurs when two people are at the same time creditors and debtors of one another (Article 1497 of the UCC). The compensation takes place by ministerio legis (by operation of the law), and it generates that both debts extinguish in the same amount (Article 1498 of the UCC).

548. For the compensation of two debts to take place *ipso jure*, it is required that: (a) the object of both be of the same kind, (b) both are liquid, (c) both debts are due, and (d) each of the debtors is the one that holds the debt (Article 1499 of the UCC). Compensation is not allowed for alimony debtors (Article 1510 of the UCC), and in the cases of debts originated in the lack of devolution of a thing given due to a contract of bailment, or loan (Article 1509 of the UCC).

§4. DIRECT CLAIM (POSSIBILITY CREATED BY STATUTE LAW TO CLAIM PAYMENT DIRECTLY FROM THE DEBTOR OF ONE'S DEBTOR)

549. The direct claim refers to the action allowed by law to a creditor, to file an action against the debtor of his debtor. In this case, the creditor does not occupy the position of his debtor, but acts in his own name.

550. A case of direct claim in Uruguayan law is the one granted by Article 12 of Law 18,412. This law establishes the obligation of the owners of motor vehicles to hire an automobile mandatory insurance (SOA). Until this law, when a motor vehicle caused harm to a person, he had to sue the author of the harm, and the insurance company would appear in Court, representing the defendant, or as a third party interested in the outcome of the proceeding. But after this law, the victim of a harm caused by a motor vehicle can ask for a compensation directly from the insurance company.

551. Another case of direct claim is the one established in Article 1851 of the CC, which allows the construction workers, carpenters, and other workers who have been hired by a businessman for the construction of a building to sue directly the owner of the project for the amount he owes the businessman in charge of it.

552. Finally, another case is the one established in Article 1821 of the CC, which allows the lessor to collect from the sublessee, the amount the lessee owes him (but the sublessee will only be obliged up to the sum he owes the lessee).

Selected Bibliography

Books

General Works

Berdaguer, Jaime, "The Obligation," Vol. I, Editorial Fundacion de Cultura Universitaria, Montevideo,

Caffera, Gerardo, El contrato de Fideicomiso, análisis de la ley Uruguaya 17.703, Asociación de Escribanos del Uruguay, 2003

Diez-Picazo, Luis, and Gullon, Antonio, "Sistema de Derecho Civil," Vol. III, 7th Edition, Editorial Tecnos

Fabbrini, Fabrizio, Novissimo Digesto Italiano, T. XX, Unione Tipografico—Editrice Torinese, Torino, 1982.

Gamarra, Jorge, Tratado de Derecho Civil Uruguayo, Vol. II, 3rd Edition, Fundación de Cultura Universitaria, 1989

Gamarra, Jorge, *Tratado de Derecho Civil Uruguayo*, Vol. VIII, Montevideo, Fundación de Cultura Universitaria, 2010

García Maynez, "Introducción al estudio del derecho," México: Porrúa, 1988 México: Porrúa, 1988 pág. 372

Guillot Muñoz, Alvaro, Comentarios del Codigo Civil. De la Posesión y de la Reivindicación, cited by Howard, Walter, *Modos de Adquirir.*

Howard, Walter, *Modos de Adquirir*, Montevideo, Editorial of the University of Montevideo, 2002.

Peirano Facio, Jorge, *Curso de Obligaciones*, Volume I, Montevideo, Fundación de Cultura Universitaria, 1957

Plá Rodríguez, Americo "Los principios del Derecho del trabajo," 2nd Edition, Fundación de Cultura Universitaria

Rodriguez Olivera, Nuri, *Titulos Valores Ley 14,701*, Montevideo, Editorial Acali, 1985.

Sayagues Laso, Enrique, *Tratado de Derecho Administrativo*, Editorial Fundación de Cultura Universitaria, 1988.

Tome, Miguel Angel, "Negocios Jurídicos Simulados y Fraudulentos," FCU, Montevideo, 2008.

Vescovi, Enrique, *Introducción al Derecho,* 17th edn. Montevideo, Idea, 1992.

Venturini, Beatriz, and others, Manual de Contratos, Volumes I and II, Montevideo, Editorial of the University of Montevideo, 2011

Selected Bibliography

Yglesias, Arturo, *Derecho de l as Cosas*, Vol. I, Montevideo, Fundación de Cultura Universitaria, 1997

Monographs

Lanziano Washington: Estudios de Derecho de superficie y Propiedad Horizontal, pág. 62, cited by Susana Cambiasso, in her article "El Derecho de superficie en el Derecho Uruguayo," published online at: http://www.acaderc.org.ar/doctrina/articulos/el-derecho-de-superficie-en-el-derecho-uruguayo

Rodriguez Olivera, Nuri and Lopez, Carlos, *Régimen Jurídico del Contrato de Leasing*, published online at http://www.derechocomercial.edu.uy/ClaseContCrUsoRegimen.htm.

Salgado, Sonia and Tellechea, Andrea, Aportes para un Estudio de Títulos, page 123, published online at http://www.fder.edu.uy/material/salgado-tellechea_aportes-para-un-estudio-de-titulos.pdf. This monograph was coordinated by Dora Bagdassarian.

Salis Lino, Superficie (Diritto vigente). En Novisimo Digesto Italiano. T. XVIII. Pág. 948, cited by Lanziano Washington: Estudios de Derecho de Superficie y Propiedad Horizontal, cited by Susana Cambiasso, in her article "El Derecho de superficie en el Derecho Uruguayo," published online at: http://www.acaderc.org.ar/doctrina/articulos/el-derecho-de-superficie-en-el-derecho-uruguayo

Articles and Notes

Achaval, Estefania and others, "Algunas Reflexiones sobre el Régimen de la Propiedad Horizontal en el Derecho Positivo Uruguayo," *CADE*, Volume 87, 2005.

Camaño Iriondo, Mario, "El derecho de preferencia del art. 35 Ley 11.029," *Revista de Derecho Agrario*, No. 4: 34.

De los Santos, Maria Laura, "Nuevo Regimen de Incorporacion a Propiedad Horizontal," published at http://www.guyer.com.uy/wp-content/uploads/2012/12/16_Propiedad-Horizontal_LSC_06_12_2012.pdf

Fernandez Reyes, Jorge, "El Derecho de Superficie en la Ley de Ordenamiento Territorial y Desarrollo Sostenible y la Materia Agraria," *CADE Doctrina y Jurisprudencia* 345, online version, 7/6/2010.

Ferreira, Hector, "The Nuts and Bolts of Uruguayan Insolvency and Bankruptcy Laws," published on the Emerging Markets Restructuring Journal of Cleary Gottlieb, Issue No 2, Fall 2016, https://www.clearygottlieb.com/~/media/organize-archive/cgsh/files/emerging-markets-restructuring-journal/emrj-issue-2-fall-2016/05-the-nuts-and-bolts-of-uruguayan-insolvency-and-bankruptcy-laws.pdf

Gutierrez, Nestor, "Protección Legal contra el Ruido y la Contaminación Acústica," published in CADE 443, 2010, Montevideo.

Iglesias, Arturo, "El número de los derechos reales, la superficie y los derechos de adquisición." *Anuario de Derecho Civil Uruguayo*, No. XXV (1994): 623

Jurisprudence

Vazquez, José, and others v. C.U.T.C.S.A., SCJ No. 246/2002 (2002)

Pedro Santana SA c. Shepley, TAC 2, 71/2014 (2014)

Instituto Nacional de Colonización v. FITESUR S.A., TAC 1, No. CED-0003-000997/2013 (2013)
García Silvera, Ivonne Graciela v. García García, María del Carmen; y otra, TAC 2, 127/2011 (2011)
Winterbotham Fiduciaria S.A. y otro c/ Loygreen S.A., TAC 6, No. 0006-000026/2014 (2014)
Roca, Juan Jose v. Davyt Bouissa, Ana Elena and others, SCJ, 219/2001 (2001)

Webpages

Webpage of the Investment and Export Promotion Institute: http://www.uruguayxxi.gub.uy/en/reliable-country/
Webpage of the Ministry of Housing, Territorial Ordinance and Environment: http://www.mvotma.gub.uy/planificacion-departamental/item/10002805-instrumentos-de-ordenamiento-territorial.html
Webpage of the Public Database of National Jurisprudence of the Judicial Power of Uruguay: http://bjn.poderjudicial.gub.uy/BJNPUBLICA/busquedaSimple.seam
Webpage of the Legal Database of Uruguay: http://www.impo.com.uy/cgi-bin/bases/consultaBasesBS.cgi

Selected Bibliography

Index

The numbers here refer to paragraph numbers.

www.ingramcontent.com/pod-product-compliance
Ingram Content Group UK Ltd.
Pitfield, Milton Keynes, MK11 3LW, UK
UKHW020147290926
15471UKWH00004B/747

9 789403 547541